Hard Times
1930-1940

TIME LIFE BOOKS ®

This Fabulous Century

Hard Times
1930-1940

By the Editors of TIME-LIFE BOOKS

Time-Life Books, Alexandria, Virginia

Time-Life Books is a division of Time Life Inc.,
a wholly owned subsidiary of
THE TIME INC. BOOK COMPANY

TIME-LIFE BOOKS

Managing Editor: Thomas H. Flaherty
Director of Editorial Resources: Elise D. Ritter-Clough
Director of Photography and Research: John Conrad Weiser
Editorial Board: Dale M. Brown, Roberta Conlan, Laura Foreman,
Lee Hassig, Jim Hicks, Blaine Marshall, Rita Thievon Mullin,
Henry Woodhead

PUBLISHER: Joseph J. Ward

Associate Publisher: Ann M. Mirabito
Editorial Director: Russ Adams
Marketing Director: Anne Everhart
Director of Design: Louis Klein
Production Manager: Prue Harris
Supervisor of Quality Control: James King

EDITORIAL OPERATIONS
Production: Celia Beattie
Library: Louise D. Forstall
Computer Composition: Deborah G. Tait (Manager),
Monika D. Thayer, Janet Barnes Syring, Lillian Daniels

THIS FABULOUS CENTURY

SERIES EDITOR: Ezra Bowen
Editorial Staff for *1930-1940: Hard Times*
Picture Editor: Mary Y. Steinbauer
Designer: John R. Martinez
Assistant Designer: Jean Lindsay Morein
Staff Writers: Tony Chiu, Sam Halper, Anne Horan, Lucille Schulberg,
Gerald Simons, Bryce S. Walker, Edmund White
Researchers: Alice Baker, Terry Drucker, Marcia A. Gillespie, Helen
Greenway, Helen M. Hinkle, Carol Isenberg, Nancy J. Jacobsen, Mary
Kay Moran, Nancy C. Shappelle, Victoria Winterer, Johanna Zacharias
Design Assistant: Anne B. Landry

CORRESPONDENTS: Elisabeth Kraemer-Singh (Bonn), Maria Vin-
cenza Aloisi (Paris), Ann Natanson (Rome). Valuable assistance was also
provided by: Norman Airey, J. Patrick Barker, Jane Beatty, Pam Burke,
Patricia Chandler, Jane Estes, Murray J. Gart, Juliane Greenwalt,
Blanche Hardin, Ned Judge, George Karas, Lucille Larkin, Frank Leem-
ing Jr., Joyce Leviton, Benjamin Lightman, Jerry Madden, Holland Mc-
Combs, Doris O'Neill, Jane Rieker, William Roberts, Gayle Rosenberg,
Rod Van Every, Nelson Wadsworth, Earl Zarbin.

LIBRARY OF CONGRESS CATALOGING IN PUBLICATION DATA
This fabulous century / by the editors of Time-Life Books.
    p.   cm.
   Includes bibliographical references and index.
   Contents: — v. [4] 1930-1940 : hard times.
   ISBN 0-8094-8204-5
   1. United States—Social life and customs—20th century. 2. United
States—Popular culture—History—20th century. 3. United States—
Social life and customs—20th century—Pictorial works. 4. United
States—Description and travel—Views.   I. Time-Life Books.
E161.T55   1991
973.917'0222—dc20   91-10553
                      CIP

Contents

America 1930-1940

Bathing beauties at Catalina Island, California, 1933.

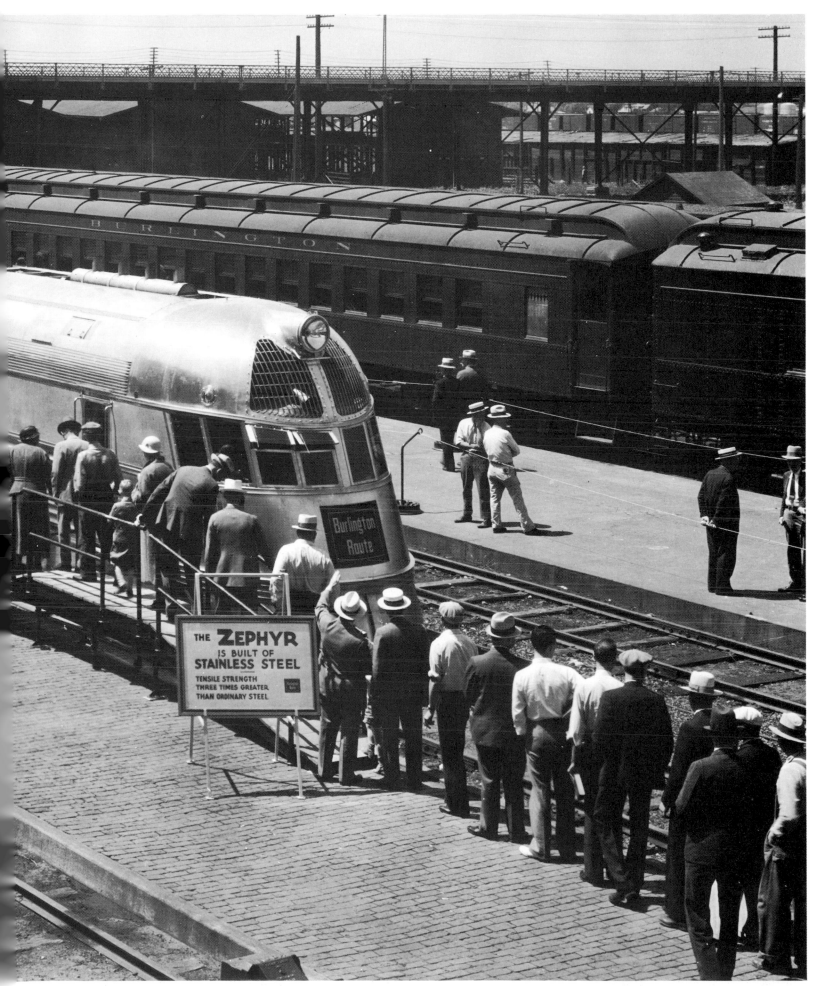

Public tour of America's first streamlined train, Lincoln, Nebraska, 1934.

Midwest newsstand, November 1938.

Celebrating the repeal of Prohibition, December 1933.

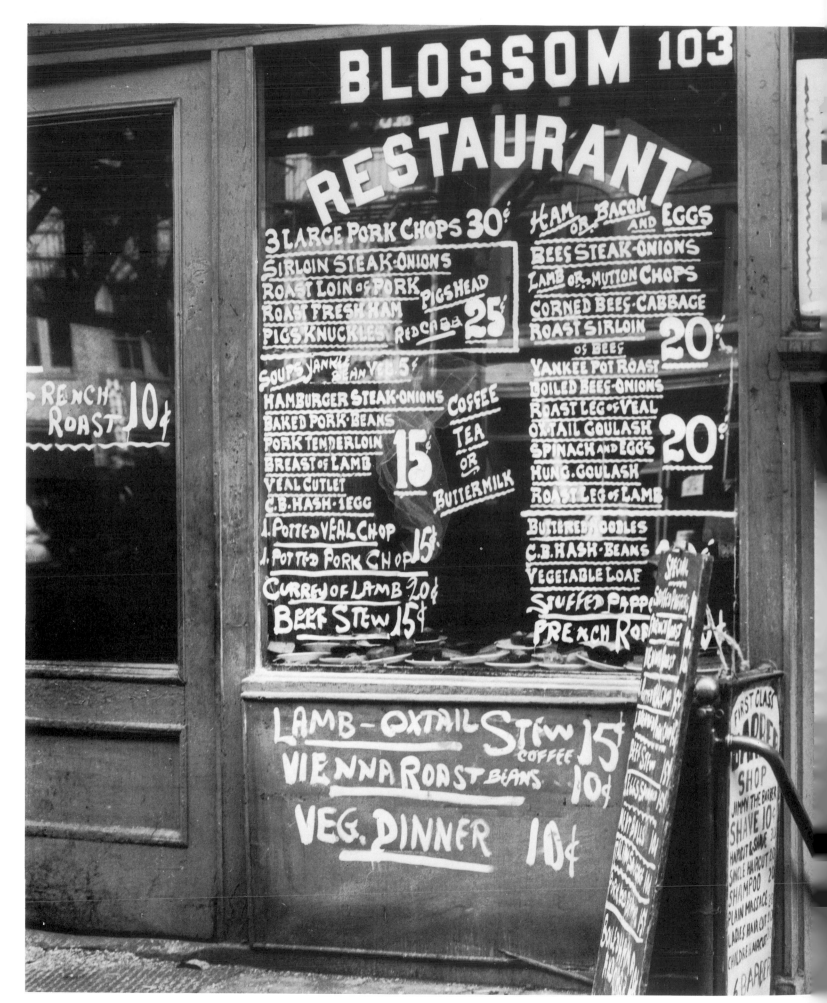

Shop owner in New York's Bowery, 1935.

17   "*Dollar Day*" *sale at Filene's Department Store, Boston, 1938.*

Afternoon dance at a Miami, Florida, trailer camp, 1938.

Bedroom suite, Hollywood, California, about 1937.

A poster urged Americans to help the economy. "How'd they expect us to buy autos when we can't buy food?" a tinsmith asked.

Journey through the Lean Years

We are the first nation in the history of the world
to go to the poor house in an automobile.

WILL ROGERS

Herbert Hoover stumbled out of bed at six o'clock on the chill, gray morning of March 4, 1933, to be told that on his last day as President the banking system of the United States had collapsed. The news was the final defeat in a disastrous term of office, and the weary President answered, "We are at the end of our string. There is nothing more we can do." His mournful words echoed the spirit of the nation and concluded the frantic but unavailing course it had taken under the outgoing President.

Not quite three and a half years had passed since the stock market crash had plunged the United States, and most of the world, into the worst economic debacle in Western memory. Industrial output was now less than half the 1929 figure. The number of unemployed, although difficult to count accurately, had mounted to something between 13 and 15 million, or a record high of 25 per cent of the labor force—and the unemployed had 30 million mouths to feed besides their own. Hourly wages had dropped 60 per cent since 1929, white-collar salaries 40 per cent. Farmers were getting five cents a pound for cotton and less than 50 cents a bushel for wheat.

The stark statistics gave no real picture of the situation —of the pitiful men who sold apples on city street corners; of the long lines of haggard men and women who waited for dry bread or thin soup, meager sustenance dispensed by private and municipal charities; of the bloated bellies of starving children; of distraught farmers blocking roads to dump milk cans in a desperate effort to force up the price of milk. "They say blockading the highway's illegal," said an Iowa farmer. "I says, 'Seems to me there was a Tea Party in Boston that was illegal too.'"

Everywhere there was hunger. "We saw a crowd of some 50 men fighting over a barrel of garbage which had been set outside the back door of a restaurant," said an observer in Chicago. "American citizens fighting for scraps of food like animals!" As though they had not troubles enough, millions of workless, hungry and beaten people lacked even the Constitutional right to vote. In September 1932 the city officials of Lewiston, Maine, voted to bar all welfare recipients from the polls; at least 10 states from Massachusetts to Oregon had poll tax and property requirements beyond the reach of Depression victims; and a million or more nomads, wandering about the country, lacked the residency requirements for voting.

For all that, scores of the surviving rich and far too many of those in public office seemed blind to the mis-

Annual Earnings: 1932 to 1934

AIRLINE PILOT	$8,000.00
AIRLINE STEWARDESS	$1,500.00
APARTMENT HOUSE SUPERINTENDENT	$1,500.00
BITUMINOUS COAL MINER	$723.00
BUS DRIVER	$1,373.00
CHAUFFEUR	$624.00
CIVIL SERVICE EMPLOYEE	$1,284.00
COLLEGE TEACHER	$3,111.00
CONSTRUCTION WORKER	$907.00
DENTIST	$2,391.00
DEPARTMENT STORE MODEL	$936.00
DOCTOR	$3,382.00
DRESSMAKER	$780.00
ELECTRICAL WORKER	$1,559.00
ENGINEER	$2,520.00
FIRE CHIEF (city of 30,000 to 50,000)	$2,075.00
HIRED FARM HAND	$216.00
HOUSEMOTHER–BOYS' SCHOOL	$780.00
LAWYER	$4,218.00
LIVE-IN MAID	$260.00
MAYOR (city of 30,000 to 50,000)	$2,317.00
PHARMACEUTICAL SALESMAN	$1,500.00
POLICE CHIEF (city of 30,000 to 50,000)	$2,636.00
PRIEST	$831.00
PUBLIC SCHOOL TEACHER	$1,227.00
PUBLICITY AGENT	$1,800.00
RAILROAD EXECUTIVE	$5,064.00
RAILROAD CONDUCTOR	$2,729.00
REGISTERED NURSE	$936.00
SECRETARY	$1,040.00
STATISTICIAN	$1,820.00
STEELWORKER	$422.87
STENOGRAPHER-BOOKKEEPER	$936.00
TEXTILE WORKER	$435.00
TYPIST	$624.00
UNITED STATES CONGRESSMAN	$8,663.00
WAITRESS	$520.00

erable realities of the Depression. "I do not believe in any quick or spectacular remedies for the ills from which the world is suffering, nor do I share the belief that there is fundamentally anything wrong with the social system," said multimillionaire Andrew Mellon, former Secretary of the Treasury.

"There is something about too much prosperity that ruins the fiber of the people," said diplomat Dwight Morrow when he was running for governor of New Jersey. "People are growing more courteous in business, and often more reasonable at home, thoughtless women especially," editorialized *The Literary Digest*, adding: "Unappreciative wives who were indifferent to their husbands and neglected their homes have become tame and cautious." The Metropolitan Life Insurance Company had a grimmer observation. It reported that 20,000 persons committed suicide in 1931, a figure that far exceeded the legendary suicides of the months following the Crash.

Hoover himself plugged away with firm-jawed righteousness that won him no thanks from the hopeless millions. "Economic depression cannot be cured by legislative action or executive pronouncement," he said. Anxiously seeking some other solution, he was at his desk from 8:30 in the morning till late at night, with 15 minutes off for lunch, drafting proposals, breaking dozens of pencil points in his urgency. He pumped two billion dollars into the banks and investment houses of Wall Street through the Reconstruction Finance Corporation. But what was that to the white-collar worker whose life savings had been wiped out in the failure of his local bank? He proposed the appropriation of money "for the purpose of seed and feed for animals" in the drought-stricken farm belt. But the farmer's children went hungry and Hoover denounced as a "dole" the granting of money and food to human beings. He spent hours on the telephone picking brains and seeking support for this idea and that, and called meeting after meeting of industrial and financial moguls. The latter habit moved the Baltimore *Evening Sun* to deride one such gathering as the President's "new panel of honorary pallbearers" and Representative George

Huddleston of Alabama to growl: "In the White House we have a man more interested in the pocketbooks of the rich than in the bellies of the poor."

Hoover's stand against the concept of the "dole" was shared by thousands. But otherwise he was scorned and derided by most Americans, and his administration was

---

Nothing could be worse for the general public than a Federal dole.   SILAS H. STRAWN, U.S. CHAMBER OF COMMERCE

---

so bitterly blamed for the Depression that his name became an adjective for all the manifestations of the blight.

There were Hoover blankets, old newspapers used for warmth by park-bench tenants. Hoover flags were empty pocket linings turned inside out. In the country there were Hoover hogs, the jack rabbits that impoverished farmers caught for food, and Hoover wagons, broken-down cars restored to locomotion with the help of mules.

In cities all over the country there were Hoovervilles, squalid villages that sprang up in the vacant lots where the homeless sheltered themselves in sheds made of packing boxes and scrap metal while they foraged about the city for food; New York had at least two Hoovervilles, one below Riverside Drive and the other in Central Park.

The biggest Hooverville of all sprang up on the President's doorstep in Washington, and from it emanated one of the sorest incidents of Hoover's luckless administration. Veterans of World War I had for some time been pleading for advance payment of a war bonus they were due to receive in 1945. In the spring of 1932 an unemployed Oregon canner, Walter W. Waters, conceived the idea of staging a sort of one-shot veterans' lobby in Congress. All through the month of June, war veterans and their families streamed into Washington, by freight car, by truck and on foot, until they numbered 20,000.

The Bonus Expeditionary Force, as the veterans called themselves, found a hostile city; the only official who made them welcome was Brigadier General Pelham D. Glassford, chief of the Washington police. He provided them with makeshift housing in empty government build-

ings, and when those ran out he allowed them to camp in a swampy area across the Potomac. He persuaded the Army to lend them tents and cots, and rigged up an Army field kitchen to provide them with food. He ordered his own men to treat them humanely, and he himself rode from site to site on a motorcycle, giving smiles and encouragement, calling the hopeful veterans "my boys."

Predictably, the Senate voted against the bonus, and most of the veterans left Washington to go home. But some 8,600 with no homes to go to stayed on in their Washington Hoovervilles, jarring the nerves of the President, who was by then engaged in a doomed campaign for reelection. Chains went up on the White House gates, guards patrolled the grounds night and day, and the streets were closed to traffic. On the morning of July 28, Glassford got word from the "highest authority" that the bonus marchers must quit the government buildings.

Glassford's cordial treatment of the men now stood him in good stead. He paid the veterans another visit and persuaded them to move out of their own accord, a request they set out to obey in return for his favors to them.

The evacuation proceeded all through the day, but the "highest authority" was not satisfied. Late in the afternoon General Douglas MacArthur, Chief of Staff of the United States Army, marched up Pennsylvania Avenue, with a major named Dwight D. Eisenhower at his side.

Federal feeding would set a most dangerous precedent. It would be too dangerously like the dole, which paralyzed British labor.

SCHENECTADY *UNION-STAR*

They headed a parade of infantry, cavalry, machine guns, tanks and trucks. That formidable array of weaponry, abetted by tear gas bombs and sabers, scattered the few who remained. Not content with routing the squatters from the empty government buildings, the troops pursued fleeing women, children and even a few legless veterans across the river to the swamp, where they burned the shacks that had been home to the pitiful ragtags for more than a month. In the last burst of gas bombs at midnight, an 11-month-old baby reportedly died, and the remnants of the veterans' march joined the throngs of Americans whom the Depression had already turned into nomads.

"A challenge to the authority of the United States Government has been met," said Hoover. But the episode cost him dear. The marchers never forgave him; neither did hundreds of thousands of sympathizers, who helped to vote Hoover out of office three months later.

The following year a second veterans' army assembled in Washington. Though it too failed to get the bonus payment, it received a far gentler White House recognition, in the form of an appearance by Eleanor Roosevelt, the new President's wife, who walked among the men, listening to their songs and tasting their humble chow. Mrs. Roosevelt's visit was not only humanitarian; it was excellent politics. "Hoover sent the Army," cried the second crop of bonus marchers; "Roosevelt sent his wife."

That shrewd combination of practical politics and instinct for the common touch was to be the hallmark of the new administration, the one that was to leave its

---

I can go down to the market here and buy a parrot for $2. And in one day I can teach it to say "Dole, Dole, Dole." But that parrot would never understand an economic problem.

FIORELLO H. LA GUARDIA

---

stamp on the nation and its government as the hard-times generation climbed out of the Depression. During the first 100 days of the new administration, Roosevelt's own sure-handed brand of personal leadership *(pages 114-141)* stirred the country out of its apathy and into effective action. In scarcely three months' time the government gave $500 million for cash, food and shelter to the destitute, for the first time providing federal money for relief (the feared "dole") at the very bottom of the economic ladder. A series of other programs drawn up during this same period put the government squarely into the business of economic planning on a national scale.

Roosevelt called his startling array of legislation a "New Deal" for the nation. And indeed it seemed to be. The Fed-

eral Reserve Board's index of industrial production shot up from 59 in March 1933, the month that Roosevelt took office, to 66 in April, 78 in May, 91 in June and 100 in July, just 25 points short of the 125 high registered in the boom year of 1929. When in 1936 Roosevelt campaigned across the country for re-election, he looked out over the crowds that massed to meet him, flashed his brilliant, confident smile and said with the air of a friend, "You look much better than you did four years ago," and the people cried in answer, "God bless you, Mr. President!"

Despite a business setback in 1937-1938, by 1939 the gross national product had climbed to $91 billion, an increase of more than 60 per cent over the black days of 1933. As one bright promise of new prosperity, in October of 1939 the Du Pont Company put on sale in Wilmington 4,000 pairs of stockings made of a new fabric called nylon. It was the first fully man-made fiber and represented an endeavor of such potential that even in the Depression Du Pont was willing to spend $27 million developing it. Some wag claimed that the odd name for the new creation was an acronym made up from the words "Now You Lousy Old Nipponese," a slap at the increasingly unpopular nation of Japan, which bred the silkworms for the silk stockings that nylon would soon make obsolete. The new fabric was also a herald of dozens of wonder products that would someday be spread before millions of Americans—lightweight metal alloys, TV, synthetic detergents and frozen foods. But most Americans would have to wait to make regular use of these new inventions, for the decade that had opened with the reverberations of the financial crash was to close to the rumble of distant gunfire. In 1939 German tanks rolled into Poland; England and France declared war on Germany; and before the decade was out, the United States was tooling up for its own defense. But through the travail of the Depression that lay between the two landmarks of the crash and the Second World War, America had managed to keep its political balance, regain its economic health and reassess some of the old habits and values that had helped to lead it to the brink of these embracing cataclysms.

Depression Shopping List: 1932 to 1934

Automobiles

NEW

Pontiac coupé	$585.00
Chrysler sedan	995.00
Dodge	595.00
Studebaker	840.00
Packard	2,150.00
Chevrolet half-ton pickup truck	650.00

USED

Lincoln '27	125.00
Studebaker '30	200.00
Ford '29	57.50

Clothing

WOMEN'S

Mink coat	$585.00
Leopard coat	92.00
Cloth coat	6.98
Raincoat	2.69
Wool dress	1.95
Wool suit	3.98
Wool sweater	1.69
Silk stockings	.69
Leather shoes	1.79
Reptile leather shoes	6.00

MEN'S

Overcoat	11.00
Wool suit	10.50
Trousers	2.00
Shirt	.47
Pullover sweater	1.95
Silk necktie	.55
Suede hunting shirt	2.94
Calfskin riding boots	9.50
Golf suit	20.00
Tuxedo	25.00
Stetson hat	5.00
Shoes	3.85

Household Items

Silver plate flatware, 26-piece	$4.98
Double-bed sheets	.67
Bath towel	.24
Wool blanket	1.00
Linen tablecloth	1.00
Wool rug (9' x 12')	5.85

Appliances

Electric iron	$2.00
Electric coffee percolator	1.39
Electric mixer	9.95
Vacuum cleaner	18.75
Electric washing machine	47.95
Gas stove	23.95
Electric portable sewing machine	24.95
Copper lamp	1.95

Furniture

Dining room set, 8-piece	$46.50
Bedroom set, 3-piece	49.95
Lounge chair	19.95
Double bed and spring mattress	14.95
Bridge table	1.00
Colonial walnut secretary	54.00
Mahogany coffee table	10.75
Chippendale mahogany sofa	135.00
Louis XV walnut dining table	124.00
Wing chair	39.00
Grand piano	395.00

Miscellaneous

Dental filling	$1.00
Tooth paste (large)	.25
Coty face powder	1.50
L'Aimant perfume, ¼ oz.	1.00
Cultivated Oriental pearls	35.00
Razor blades (10)	.49
Cigarettes	.15
Cigarette lighter	.39
Pipe	.83
Alarm clock	2.00
Fountain pen	1.00
Briefcase	1.00
Console radio	49.95
Electric shaver	15.00
Desk typewriter	19.75
Movie camera, 8 mm.	29.50
Kodak Box Brownie	2.50
Automobile tire	6.20
Gasoline (per gallon)	.18

Toys

Doll carriage	$4.98
Sled	1.45
Tricycle	3.98
Two-wheeled bike	10.95
Fielder's glove and ball	1.25
Catcher's mitt	1.19
Leather basketball	1.00
BB air rifle	.79

Food

Sirloin steak (per lb.)	$0.29
Round steak (per lb.)	.26
Rib roast (per lb.)	.22
Bacon (per lb.)	.22
Ham (per lb.)	.31
Leg of lamb (per lb.)	.22
Chicken (per lb.)	.22
Pork chops (per lb.)	.20
Salmon (16 oz. can)	.19
Milk (per qt.)	.10
Butter (per lb.)	.28
Margarine (per lb.)	.13
Eggs (per doz.)	.29
Cheese (per lb.)	.24
Bread (20 oz. loaf)	.05
Coffee (per lb.)	.26
Sugar (per lb.)	.05
Rice (per lb.)	.06
Potatoes (per lb.)	.02
Tomatoes (16 oz. can)	.09
Oranges (per doz.)	.27
Bananas (per lb.)	.07
Onions (per lb.)	.03
Cornflakes (8 oz. package)	.08

Real Estate

Modern house, 6 rooms 2-car garage, Detroit	$2,800.00
English cottage, 8 rooms, 3 baths, 1 ballroom, Seattle	4,250.00
Italian villa, 12 rooms, Westchester, N.Y.	17,000.00
Spanish stucco, 7 rooms, Beverly Hills	5,000.00

Travel

AIR

New York to Chicago, round trip	$86.31
Chicago to Los Angeles, round trip	207.00

RAIL

Chicago to San Francisco round trip, 16 days in San Francisco	80.50
New York City to Scarsdale, N.Y., monthly commuter ticket	10.39

SEA

Tour of Europe, 60 days, 11 countries	495.00
Bermuda-Havana-Nassau, cruise, 10 days	110.00
Around the world, 85 days, 14 countries	749.00
San Francisco to Hawaii, round trip	220.00
New York to California via Panama Canal	120.00

Radio

The cast of "Gangbusters" blasts away to open a new episode.

On the Air

There are three things which I shall never forget about America—the Rocky Mountains,

the Statue of Liberty and Amos 'n' Andy.   GEORGE BERNARD SHAW, 1933

Every weekday evening from 7:00 to 7:15 p.m., telephone use all over the country dropped 50 per cent, car thieves had an easy time on empty streets, and many movie theaters shut off their projectors to pipe in pure radio while some 30 million Americans—including President Roosevelt—tuned in to *Amos 'n' Andy (page 38)*. Such devotion to a comedy serial—created in black-voice by a pair of white vaudevillians, Freeman Gosden and Charles Correll—was typical of radio audiences in the '30s. The big box in the living room was everybody's ticket to adventure, laughter, sweet music and romance.

People listened for the openers of their favorite shows the way little children listened for the sound of father's car in the driveway. Starting not long after breakfast each morning, serial dramas kept housewives intrigued all day: "Can this girl from a mining town in the West find happiness as the wife of a wealthy and titled Englishman?" the announcer asked at the beginning of *Our Gal Sunday*. Everyone hoped so but no one knew for sure.

During supper the family listened to the news, and then sat back to a marvelous, manufactured world in which you supplied the pictures while the radio brought in the sound. Millions of meek men joined the cops to patrol the dangerous streets of *Gangbusters*. Folksy types eased down in their armchairs when Kate Smith belted out her theme song, "When the Moon Comes Over the Mountain." And comedy fans giggled at Edgar Bergen and Charlie McCarthy. Never mind that Charlie was a ventriloquist's dummy. He seemed so real that the King of Sweden, Winston Churchill and Hollywood's Louis B. Mayer all extended their hands to him upon being introduced.

Real drama came into homes, too. Radio reporters put their shiny, wagon-wheel microphones before the lips of newsmakers and let listeners hear Lou Gehrig when the great ballplayer, dying of amyotrophic lateral sclerosis, said in a low, clear voice before 60,000 at Yankee Stadium, "I consider myself the luckiest man on the face of the earth." Other tears fell when Edward VIII of England renounced his throne for the Baltimore divorcée Wally Simpson, "the woman I love." Americans stayed glued to their radios while commentator H.V. Kaltenborn told of the dying days of peace in Europe during his marathon news broadcast *(page 39)*. But when actor Orson Welles simulated a news broadcast of a fictional invasion by men from Mars, thousands of Americans poured into the streets in panic, sure the end of the world had come.

Kate Smith, the hefty "Songbird of the South," with her cheery "Hello everybody!" was heard by some 16 million fans every Thursday at eight.

Highlights of the Six-Day Week

OZZIE NELSON AND HARRIET HILLIARD

GEORGE BURNS AND GRACIE ALLEN

FIBBER MC GEE AND MOLLY

	Sunday	Monday	Tuesday
7:00	NBC–*Red*: JELL-O PROGRAM—Jack Benny, Mary Livingstone, Kenny Baker, Don Wilson, Andy Devine, Phil Harris' orchestra NBC–*Blue*: POPULAR CLASSICS—H. Leopold Spitalny CBS: JOAN AND KERMIT—dramatic serial MBS: HAWAII CALLS	NBC–*Red*: AMOS 'N' ANDY—sketch NBC–*Blue*: MUSIC IS MY HOBBY—guests CBS: JUST ENTERTAINMENT MBS: FULTON LEWIS, JR.—Washington news commentator NBC–*Red*: UNCLE EZRA'S RADIO STATION (7:15)—Pat Barrett	NBC–*Red*: AMOS 'N' ANDY—sketch NBC–*Blue*: EASY ACES—comedy sketch CBS: JUST ENTERTAINMENT MBS: FULTON LEWIS, JR.—Washington news commentator NBC–*Blue*: MR. KEEN, TRACER OF LOST PERSONS (7:15)—dramatic serial. Bennett Kilpatrick
7:30	NBC–*Red*: INTERESTING NEIGHBORS—Jerry Belcher, interviewer NBC–*Blue*: BAKERS' BROADCAST—Feg Murray, Harriet Hilliard, Ozzie Nelson's orchestra CBS: PHIL BAKER—Beetle and Bottle, Bradley's orchestra MBS: HOLLYWOOD WHISPERS—George Fischer	NBC–*Red*: SOLOIST NBC–*Blue*: ROSE MARIE—song stylist CBS: EDDIE CANTOR'S CAMEL CARAVAN—Benny Goodman's Quartet, Bert Gordon, Walter King, Fairchild's orchestra	NBC–*Red*: BY CANDLELIGHT CBS: SECOND HUSBAND—serial, Helen Menken MBS: HEADLINES—news dramatization
8:00	NBC–*Red*: CHASE AND SANBORN PROGRAM—Don Ameche, Edgar Bergen, John Carter, Dorothy Lamour, Stroud Twins, Armbruster's orchestra NBC–*Blue*: SPY AT LARGE—dramatic serial CBS: ST. LOUIS BLUES MBS: THE WOR FORUM—S. Theodore Granik	NBC–*Red*: BURNS AND ALLEN—Tony Martin, Garber's orchestra NBC–*Blue*: RUBY NEWMAN'S ORCHESTRA CBS: YOU SAID IT!—Connie Boswell, Ted Husing, Himber's orchestra MBS: ORCHESTRA	NBC–*Red*: JOHNNY PRESENTS RUSS MORGAN AND HIS ORCHESTRA—Jack Johnstone's "Thrill of the Week" NBC–*Blue*: ENRIC MADRIGUERA AND HIS ORCHESTRA CBS: BIG TOWN—Edward G. Robinson, Claire Trevor, dramatization MBS: ORCHESTRA
8:30	NBC–*Blue*: SONGS WE REMEMBER—Gill's orchestra CBS: LYN MURRAY'S MUSICAL GAZETTE MBS: CHARIOTEERS MBS: NEWS TESTERS (8:45)—Leonard M. Leonard	NBC–*Red*: VOICE OF FIRESTONE—Richard Crooks, Margaret Speaks, Wallenstein's orchestra, guests NBC–*Blue*: THOSE WE LOVE—dramatic serial, Nan Gray, Owen Davis, Jr., Richard Cromwell, Donald Woods CBS: PICK AND PAT—comedy and music MBS: RAYMOND GRAM SWING—commentator	NBC–*Red*: LADY ESTHER SERENADE—Wayne King's orchestra NBC–*Blue*: INFORMATION PLEASE—Clifton Fadiman, John Erskine, John Kiernan and others CBS: AL JOLSON—Martha Raye, Parkyakarkus, Victor Young's orchestra, guests MBS: THE GREEN HORNET—dramatization
9:00	NBC–*Red*: MANHATTAN MERRY-GO-ROUND—Rachel Carlay, Pierre Le Kreeun, Donnie's orchestra NBC–*Blue*: HOLLYWOOD PLAYHOUSE—Tyrone Power, guests CBS: FORD SUNDAY EVENING HOUR	NBC–*Red*: MUSIC FOR MODERNS NBC–*Blue*: NOW AND THEN—orchestra CBS: LUX RADIO THEATRE—Cecil B. De Mille, guests, drama MBS: ORCHESTRA	NBC–*Red*: VOX POP—Parks Johnson, Wallace Butterworth NBC–*Blue*: HORACE HEIDT AND HIS ALEMITE BRIGADIERS—Lysbeth Hughes, Yvonne King CBS: WATCH THE FUN GO BY—Al Pearce, Nick Lucas, Hoff's orchestra MBS: ORCHESTRA
9:30	NBC–*Red*: AMERICAN ALBUM OF FAMILIAR MUSIC—Frank Munn, Jean Dickenson, Haenschen's orchestra NBC–*Blue*: JERGENS PROGRAM—Walter Winchell, news commentator MBS: ORCHESTRA NBC–*Blue*: WELCH PRESENTS IRENE RICH (9:45)—dramatization	NBC–*Red*: TALES OF GREAT RIVERS NBC–*Blue*: PAUL MARTIN AND HIS MUSIC MBS: THE WITCH'S TALE—Alonzo Deen Cole, Marie O'Flynn	NBC–*Red*: FIBBER McGEE AND MOLLY—Jim Jordan, Clark Dennis, Betty Winkler, Mills' orchestra NBC–*Blue*: NBC JAMBOREE—Don McNeill, Sylvia Clark, Fran Allison, Little Jackie Heller, Bill Thompson CBS: BENNY GOODMAN'S SWING SCHOOL MBS: MUSIC BY—guest artists
10:00	NBC–*Red*: HOUR OF CHARM—Phil Spitalny's All Girl orchestra NBC–*Blue*: NORMAN CLOTIER'S ORCHESTRA CBS: GRAND CENTRAL STATION—dramatic sketch	NBC–*Red*: CONTENTED PROGRAM—Opal Craven, Marek Weber's orchestra NBC–*Blue*: MAGNOLIA BLOSSOMS—Fisk Jubilee Choir CBS: WAYNE KING'S ORCHESTRA	NBC–*Red*: BELIEVE IT OR NOT—Robert L. Ripley, Rolfe's orchestra CBS: TIME TO SHINE—Hal Kemp's orchestra, Judy Starr, Bob Allen
10:30	NBC–*Red*: SYMPHONIC VARIATIONS—Walter Logan's orchestra NBC–*Blue*: CHEERIO—talk and music CBS: HEADLINES AND BYLINES—H. V. Kaltenborn, Bob Trout, Erwin Canham—news commentators	NBC–*Red*: FOR MEN ONLY NBC–*Blue*: NATIONAL RADIO FORUM—guest speaker CBS: LET FREEDOM RING—dramatizations MBS: HENRY WEBER'S PAGEANT OF MELODY	NBC–*Red*: JIMMIE FIDLER'S HOLLYWOOD GOSSIP CBS: RAY HEATHERTON—songs MBS: ORCHESTRA NBC–*Red*: DALE CARNEGIE (10:45)—How To Win Friends and Influence People
11:00	NBC–*Red*: DANCE MUSIC NBC–*Blue*: PRESS-RADIO NEWS; ORCHESTRA CBS: ORCHESTRA MBS: ORCHESTRA	NETWORK SIGN OFF (Local programming only)	NBC–*Red*: DANCE MUSIC NBC–*Blue*: DANCE MUSIC CBS: DANCE MUSIC MBS: DEVELOPMENT OF MUSIC

As this schedule for the week of June 5, 1938, indicates, the big evening shows of radio's week ran from Sunday through Friday on four networks (t

Wednesday	KAY KYSER	Thursday	MAJOR BOWES	Friday	MR. FIRST NIGHTER

Wednesday	Thursday	Friday
NBC–*Red*: AMOS 'N' ANDY—sketch NBC–*Blue*: EASY ACES—comedy sketch NBC–*Red*: UNCLE EZRA'S RADIO STATION (7:15)—Pat Barrett NBC–*Blue*: MR. KEEN, TRACER OF LOST PERSONS (7:15)—dramatic serial, Bennett Kilpatrick	NBC–*Red*: AMOS 'N' ANDY—sketch NBC–*Blue*: EASY ACES—comedy sketch NBC–*Blue*: MR. KEEN, TRACER OF LOST PERSONS (7:15)—dramatic serial CBS: HOLLYWOOD SCREEN SCOOPS (7:15)—George McCall MBS: OUTDOORS WITH BOB EDGE (7:15)	NBC–*Red*: AMOS 'N' ANDY—sketch NBC–*Blue*: THE FOUR OF US CBS: JUST ENTERTAINMENT MBS: FULTON LEWIS, JR.—Washington news commentator NBC–*Blue*: STORY BEHIND THE HEADLINES (7:15)—Cesar Saerchinger
NBC–*Red*: TALES BY EDWIN C. HILL NBC–*Blue*: ROSE MARIE—song stylist NBC–*Red*: HAPPY JACK (7:45)—songs NBC–*Blue*: SCIENCE ON THE MARCH (7:45) CBS: HISTORY'S HEADLINES (7:45)	NBC–*Red*: VOCALIST NBC–*Blue*: VOCALIST CBS: ST. LOUIS BLUES MBS: HEADLINES—news dramatization	NBC–*Blue*: TALES OF EDWIN C. HILL CBS: VOCALIST NBC–*Red*: THREE ROMEOS (7:45) NBC–*Blue*: VOCALIST (7:45) CBS: SCIENCE AND SOCIETY (7:45)
NBC–*Red*: ONE MAN'S FAMILY—sketch NBC–*Blue*: ROY SHIELD'S REVUE CBS: CAVALCADE OF AMERICA—guests, Voorhees' orchestra MBS: ORCHESTRA	NBC–*Red*: ROYAL GELATIN PROGRAM—Rudy Vallee, guests NBC–*Blue*: MARCH OF TIME—news dramatizations CBS: KATE SMITH—Ted Collins, Miller's orchestra MBS: ALFRED WALLENSTEIN'S SINFONIETTA	NBC–*Red*: CITIES SERVICE CONCERT—Lucille Manners, Frank Black's orchestra NBC–*Blue*: MAURICE SPITALNY'S ORCHESTRA CBS: THE GHOST OF BENJAMIN SWEET—dramatic serial
NBC–*Red*: RALEIGH AND KOOL SHOW—Tommy Dorsey's orchestra, Edythe Wright, Jack Leonard, Paul Stewart NBC–*Blue*: HARRIET PARSONS—Hollywood commentator CBS: BEN BERNIE—Lew Lehr, Buddy Clark MBS: LET'S VISIT—Dave Driscoll, Jerry Danzig	MBS: THE GREEN HORNET—dramatization NBC–*Blue*: PIANO DUO (8:45)	NBC–*Blue*: DEATH VALLEY DAYS—dramatization CBS: PAUL WHITEMAN'S ORCHESTRA—Joan Edwards MBS: TOPICS OF THE DAY—speaker
NBC–*Red*: TOWN HALL TONIGHT—Fred Allen, Portland Hoffa, Van Steeden's orchestra NBC–*Blue*: TUNE TYPES—variety program CBS: ANDRE KOSTELANETZ—Deems Taylor, guests MBS: ORCHESTRA MBS: JOHNSON FAMILY (9:15)—sketch, with Jimmy Scribner	NBC–*Red*: GOOD NEWS OF 1938—Robert Taylor, Fannie Brice, Frank Morgan, Willson's orchestra NBC–*Blue*: TORONTO PROMENADE CONCERT CBS: MAJOR BOWES' AMATEUR HOUR MBS: THE HARMONAIRES	NBC–*Red*: WALTZ TIME—Frank Munn, Lyman's orchestra NBC–*Blue*: ROYAL CROWN REVUE—Tim and Irene, Uncle Happy, Graham McNamee, Fredda Gibson, George Olsen's orchestra CBS: HOLLYWOOD HOTEL—Louella Parsons, Frances Langford, Frank Parker, Ken Murray MBS: ORCHESTRA
NBC–*Blue*: BOSTON "POP" CONCERT CBS: THE WORD GAME—Max Eastman MBS: JAZZ NOCTURNE—Helene Daniels, Stanley's orchestra	MBS: RAY SINATRA'S MOONLIGHT RHYTHMS—Sylvia Froos, Jack Arthur	NBC–*Red*: A. L. ALEXANDER'S TRUE STORIES—dramatization NBC–*Blue*: NBC SPELLING BEE—Paul Wing MBS: WLW OPERETTA
NBC–*Red*: KAY KYSER'S MUSICAL CLASS AND DANCE NBC–*Blue*: CHOIR SYMPHONETTE CBS: GANGBUSTERS—crime dramatizations, Col. H. Norman Schwartzkopf MBS: ORCHESTRA	NBC–*Red*: KRAFT MUSIC HALL—Bing Crosby, Bob Burns, Trotter's orchestra, guests NBC–*Blue*: UNDER WESTERN SKIES CBS: ESSAYS IN MUSIC—Victor Bay's orchestra, Margaret Daum, Ruth Carhart, David Ross MBS: DRAMATIZATION	NBC–*Red*: FIRST NIGHTER—dramatization, Les Tremayne, Barbara Luddy NBC–*Blue*: PAUL MARTIN'S ORCHESTRA CBS: COLUMBIA SQUARE MBS: BAMBERGER SYMPHONY ORCHESTRA
NBC–*Blue*: NBC MINSTREL SHOW—Gene Arnold, orchestra CBS: EDGAR GUEST IN "IT CAN BE DONE"—Marion Francis Masters' orchestra MBS: MELODIES FROM THE SKY	NBC–*Blue*: NBC PROMENADE CONCERT CBS: AMERICANS AT WORK MBS: HENRY WEBER'S CONCERT REVUE	NBC–*Red*: JIMMIE FIDLER'S HOLLYWOOD GOSSIP MBS: CURTAIN TIME—dramatization CBS: AMERICAN VIEWPOINT (10:45)
NBC–*Red*: DANCE MUSIC NBC–*Blue*: DANCE MUSIC CBS: DANCE MUSIC MBS: ORCHESTRA	NBC–*Red*: SPORTS QUESTION BOX NBC–*Blue*: ORCHESTRA CBS: DUKE ELLINGTON'S ORCHESTRA NBC–*Blue*: ELZA SCHALLERT REVIEWS (11:15)—previews, guests MBS: THEATRE DIGEST (11:15)	NBC–*Red*: DANCE MUSIC NBC–*Blue*: ORCHESTRA CBS: DANCE MUSIC MBS: DANCE MUSIC

onged to NBC and were code-named Red and Blue). Saturday night most people went to the movies; a few stayed home to hear "Your Hit Parade."

Orson Welles narrated "War of the Worlds" on Halloween, 1938. Newspapers the next day reported a "tidal wave of terror that swept the nation."

Great Moments from Great Programs

From the abundant schedule of radio programs, certain moments lingered in the minds of everyone who heard them. Among the most memorable programs, some of them shown on these pages, was one that began as a Halloween joke but wound up scaring the nation half to death. On October 30, 1938, a 23-year-old producer named Orson Welles presented the radio play "Invasion from Mars," written by Howard Koch but mistakenly credited to H.G. Wells, from whose *War of the Worlds* the original idea had sprung. To make the fantasy seem credible the script simulated news broadcasts announcing that invasion forces from Mars had landed in New Jersey and were devastating the countryside with death rays. The show was brilliant radio—and America panicked.

As Welles and his cast went through the script *(excerpted below)*, thousands of people phoned their newspapers and local police to ask what they should do to avoid the invaders. In New Jersey, families tied wet cloths over their faces to escape "gas attack," piled into their cars and clogged traffic for miles. A woman in Pittsburgh, screaming "I'd rather die this way," was barely prevented from taking poison. At the end of the show, most listeners were apparently too frightened to hear Welles, chuckling, sign off by saying, "If your doorbell rings and nobody's there, that was no Martian . . . it's Halloween."

Belatedly realizing the commotion that the show had caused, CBS peppered the airwaves with reassurances that the play had been a spoof. But it took days before the last vestiges of terror had disappeared. How was it that so much of the nation went into shock at a Halloween joke? Explained one social scientist wryly: "All the intelligent people were listening to Charlie McCarthy."

MERCURY THEATRE ON THE AIR
SUNDAY, 8:00 E.S.T., CBS

ANNOUNCER: The Columbia Broadcasting System and its affiliated stations present Orson Welles and the Mercury Theatre on the Air in *War of the Worlds* by H.G. Wells.

SYNOPSIS: As the program opens, narrator Orson Welles explains, from an undetermined year in the future, that the smug people of the early 20th Century did not know about the existence of "superior intelligences" on other planets. They learned, he says, on the evening of October 30, 1938, as they were listening to their radios.

ANNOUNCER CUE
We now take you to the Meridian Room in the Hotel Park Plaza in downtown New York, where you will be entertained by the music of Ramon Raquello and his orchestra. *(Spanish theme song . . . fades)*

ANNOUNCER THREE
Good evening, ladies and gentlemen. From the Meridian Room in the Park Plaza in New York City, we bring you the music of Ramon Raquello and his orchestra. With a touch of the Spanish, Ramon Raquello leads off with "La Cumparsita." *(Piece starts playing)*

ANNOUNCER TWO
Ladies and gentlemen, we interrupt our program of dance music to bring you a special bulletin from the Intercontinental Radio News. At twenty minutes before eight, central time, Professor Farrell of the Mount Jennings Observatory, Chicago, Illinois, reports observing several explosions of incandescent gas, occurring at regular intervals on the planet Mars.

The spectroscope indicates the gas to be hydrogen and moving towards the earth with enormous velocity. Professor Pierson of the observatory at Princeton confirms Farrell's observation, and describes the phenomenon as *(Quote)* like a jet of blue flame shot from a gun. *(Unquote)* We now return you to the music of Ramon Raquello, playing for you in the Meridian Room of the Park Plaza Hotel, situated in downtown New York. *(Music plays for a few moments until piece ends . . . sound of applause)*

Now a tune that never loses favor, the ever-popular "Star Dust." Ramon Raquello and his orchestra . . . *(Music)*

ANNOUNCER TWO
Ladies and gentlemen, following on the news given in our bulletin a moment ago, the Government Meteorological Bureau has requested the large observatories of the country to keep an astronomical watch on any further disturbances occurring on the planet Mars. . . .

Ladies and gentlemen, here is the latest bulletin from the Intercontinental Radio News. Toronto, Canada: Professor Morse of Macmillan University reports observing a total of three explosions on the planet Mars, between the hours of 7:45 p.m. and 9:20 p.m., eastern standard time. This confirms earlier reports received from American observatories. Now, nearer home, comes a special announcement from Trenton, New Jersey. It is reported that at 8:50 p.m. a huge, flaming object, believed to be a meteorite, fell on a farm in the neighborhood of Grovers Mill, New Jersey, twenty-two miles from Trenton. The flash in the sky was visible within a radius of several hundred miles and the noise of the impact was heard as far north as Elizabeth.

We have dispatched a special mobile unit to the scene, and will have our commentator, Mr. Phillips, give you a word description as soon as he reaches there from Princeton. In the meantime, we take you to the Hotel Martinet in Brooklyn, where Bobby Millette and his orchestra are offering a program of dance music. (*Swing band for 20 seconds . . . then cut*)

ANNOUNCER TWO

We take you now to Grovers Mill, New Jersey. (*Crowd noises . . . police sirens*)

PHILLIPS

I wish I could convey the atmosphere . . . the background of this . . . fantastic scene. Hundreds of cars are parked in a field in back of us. Police are trying to rope off the roadway leading into the farm. But it's no use. They're breaking right through. Their headlights throw an enormous spot on the pit where the object's half-buried. Some of the more daring souls are venturing near the edge. Their silhouettes stand out. (*Faint humming sound*)

One man wants to touch the thing . . . he's having an argument with a policeman. The policeman wins. . . . Now, ladies and gentlemen, there's something I haven't mentioned in all this excitement, but it's becoming more distinct. Perhaps you've caught it already on your radio. Listen: (*Long pause*) . . . Do you hear it? It's a curious humming sound that seems to come from inside the object. I'll move the microphone nearer. Here. (*Pause*) Now we're not more than twenty-five feet away. Can you hear it now? Oh, Professor Pierson!

PIERSON

Yes, Mr. Phillips?

PHILLIPS

Can you tell us the meaning of that scraping noise inside the thing?

PIERSON

Possibly the unequal cooling of its surface.

PHILLIPS

Do you still think it's a meteor, Professor?

PIERSON

I don't know what to think. The metal casing is definitely extra-terrestrial . . . not found on this earth. Friction with the earth's atmosphere usually tears holes in a meteorite. This thing is smooth and, as you can see, of cylindrical shape.

PHILLIPS

Just a minute! Something's happening! Ladies and gentlemen, this is terrific! This end of the thing is beginning to flake off! The top is beginning to rotate like a screw! The thing must be hollow!

VOICES

She's a movin'!
Look, the darn thing's unscrewing!
Keep back, there! Keep back, I tell you.
Maybe there's men in it trying to escape!
It's red hot, they'll burn to a cinder!
Keep back there! Keep those idiots back!
(*Suddenly the clanking sound of a huge piece of falling metal*)

VOICES

She's off! The top's loose!
Look out there! Stand back!

PHILLIPS

Ladies and gentlemen, this is the most terrifying thing I have ever witnessed. . . . Wait a minute! Someone's *crawling out of the hollow top*. Some one or . . . something. I can see peering out of that black hole two luminous disks . . . are they eyes? It might be a face. It might . . . (*Shout of awe from the crowd*)

Good heavens, something's wriggling out of the shadow like a grey snake. Now it's another one, and another. They look like tentacles to me. There, I can see the thing's body. It's large as a bear and it glistens like wet leather. But that face. It . . . it's indescribable. I can hardly force myself to keep looking at it. The eyes are black and gleam like a serpent. The mouth is V-shaped with saliva dripping from its rimless lips that seem to quiver and pulsate. The monster or whatever it is can hardly move. It seems weighed down by . . . possibly gravity or something. The thing's raising up. The crowd falls back. They've seen enough. This is the most extraordinary experience. I can't find words. . . . I'm pulling this microphone with me as I talk. I'll have to stop the description until I've taken a new position. Hold on, will you please, I'll be back in a minute. (*Fade into piano*)

ANNOUNCER TWO

We are bringing you an eyewitness account of what's happening on the Wilmuth farm, Grovers Mill, New Jersey. (*More piano*)

We now return you to Carl Phillips at Grovers Mill.

PHILLIPS

Ladies and gentlemen (Am I on?). Ladies and gentlemen, here I am, back of a stone wall that adjoins Mr. Wilmuth's garden. From here I get a sweep of the whole scene. I'll give you every detail as long as I can talk. As long as I can see. More state police have arrived. They're drawing up a cordon in front of the pit, about thirty of them. No need to push the crowd back now.

They're willing to keep their distance. The captain is conferring with someone. We can't quite see who. Oh yes, I believe it's Professor Pierson. Yes, it is. Now they've parted. The professor moves around one side, studying the object, while the captain and two policemen advance with something in their hands. I can see it now. It's a white handkerchief tied to a pole . . . a flag of truce. If those creatures know what that means . . . what anything means! . . . *Wait!* Something's happening! (*Hissing sound followed by a humming that increases in intensity*)

A humped shape is rising out of the pit. I can make out a small beam of light against a mirror. What's that? There's a jet of flame springing from that mirror, and it leaps right at the advancing men. It strikes them head on! Good Lord, they're turning into flame! (*Screams and unearthly shrieks*)

Now the whole field's caught fire. (*Explosion*) The woods . . . the barns . . . the gas tanks of automobiles . . . it's spreading everywhere. It's coming this way. About twenty yards to my right. . . . (*Crash of microphone . . . then dead silence . . .*)

ANNOUNCER TWO

Ladies and gentlemen, due to circumstances beyond our control, we are unable to continue the broadcast from Grovers Mill. Evidently there's some difficulty with our field transmission. . . .

Ladies and gentlemen, I have a grave announcement to make. Incredible as it may seem, both the observations of science and the evidence of our eyes lead to the inescapable assumption that those strange beings who landed in the Jersey farmlands tonight are the vanguard of an invading army from the planet Mars. The battle which took place tonight at Grovers Mill has ended in one of the most startling defeats ever suffered by an army in modern times; seven thousand men armed with rifles and machine guns pitted against a single fighting machine of the invaders from Mars. One hundred and twenty known survivors. The rest strewn over the battle area from Grovers Mill to Plainsboro crushed and trampled to death under the metal feet of the monster, or burned to cinders by its heat-ray. The monster is now in control of the middle section of New Jersey and has effectively cut the state through its center. Communication lines are down from Pennsylvania to the Atlantic Ocean. Railroad tracks are torn and service from New York to Philadelphia discontinued except routing some of the trains through Allentown and Phoenixville. Highways to the north, south, and west are clogged with frantic human traffic. Police and army reserves are unable to control the mad flight. By morning the fugitives will have swelled Philadelphia, Camden and Trenton, it is estimated, to twice their normal population. . . .

OPERATOR THREE

This is Newark, New Jersey. . . .
This is Newark, New Jersey. . . .

Warning! Poisonous black smoke pouring in from Jersey marshes. Reaches South Street. Gas masks useless. Urge population to move into open spaces . . . automobiles use routes 7, 23, 24. . . . Avoid congested areas. Smoke now spreading over Raymond Boulevard. . . .

ANNOUNCER

I'm speaking from the roof of Broadcasting Building, New York City. The bells you hear are ringing to warn the people to evacuate the city as the Martians approach. Estimated in last two hours three million people have moved out along the roads to the north, Hutchison River Parkway still kept open for motor traffic. Avoid bridges to Long Island . . . hopelessly jammed. All communication with Jersey shore closed ten minutes ago. No more defenses. Our army wiped out . . . artillery, air force, everything wiped out. This may be the last broadcast. We'll stay here to the end.

ANNOUNCER

You are listening to a CBS presentation of Orson Welles and the Mercury Theatre on the Air in an original dramatization of *War of the Worlds* by H.G. Wells. The performance will continue after a brief intermission.

(The program resumes as Professor Pierson—a Princeton astronomer—gives his account of the denouement of the Martian invasion. He has wandered north, he reports, through devastated New Jersey, obsessed by the thought that he is the last living man on earth. On the third day of his journey he reaches Newark, which lay undemolished but seemingly devoid of life.)

PIERSON

Presently, with an odd feeling of being watched, I caught sight of something crouching in a doorway. I made a step towards it, and it rose up and became a man —a man, armed with a large knife.

STRANGER

Stop . . . Where did you come from?

PIERSON

I come from . . . many places. . . .

STRANGER

There's no food here. This is my country . . . all this end of town down to the river.

There's only food for one. . . . Which way are you going?

PIERSON

I don't know. I guess I'm looking for—for people. . . . You're in uniform.

STRANGER

What's left of it. I was in the militia—national guard. . . .

PIERSON

You and I and others . . . where are we to live when the Martians own the earth?

STRANGER

I've got it all figured out. We'll live under ground. I've been thinking about the sewers. Under New York are miles and miles of 'em. The main ones are big enough for anybody. . . . And we'll get a bunch of strong men together. No weak ones, that rubbish, out. . . .

PIERSON

Go on.

STRANGER

And we've got to make safe places for us to stay in, see; and get all the books we can —science books. That's where men like you come in, see? We'll even spy on the Martians. It may not be so much we have to learn before—just imagine this: four or five of their own fighting machines suddenly start off—heat-rays right and left and not a Martian in 'em. Not a Martian in 'em! But *men*—men who have learned the way how. It may even be in our time. Gee! Imagine having one of them lovely things with its heat-ray wide and free! We'd turn it on the Martians, we'd turn it on men. We'd bring everybody down to their knees.

PIERSON

That's your plan?

STRANGER

You and me and a few more of us we'd own the world.

PIERSON

I see.

STRANGER

Say, what's the matter? Where are you going?

PIERSON

Not to *your* world. . . . Good-bye, Stranger.

PIERSON

After parting with the artilleryman, I came at last to the Holland Tunnel. I entered that silent tube anxious to know the fate of the great city on the other side of the Hudson. Cautiously I came out of the tunnel and made my way up Canal Street.

I reached Fourteenth Street, and there again were black powder and several bodies, and an evil ominous smell from the gratings of the cellars of some of the houses. I wandered up through the thirties and

forties; I stood alone on Times Square. I caught sight of a lean dog running down Seventh Avenue with a piece of dark brown meat in his jaws, and a pack of starving mongrels at his heels. He made a wide circle around me, as though he feared I might prove a fresh competitor. I walked up Broadway in the direction of that strange powder—past silent shop windows, displaying their mute wares to empty sidewalks —past the Capitol Theatre, silent, dark —past a shooting gallery, where a row of empty guns faced an arrested line of wooden ducks. Near Columbus Circle I noticed models of 1939 motor cars in the showrooms facing empty streets. From over the top of the General Motors Building I watched a flock of black birds circling in the sky. I hurried on. I caught sight of the hood of a Martian machine, standing somewhere in Central Park, gleaming in the late afternoon sun. An insane idea! I rushed recklessly across Columbus Circle and into the Park. I climbed a small hill above the pond at Sixtieth Street. From there I could see, standing in a silent row along the Mall, nineteen of those great metal Titans, their cowls empty, their steel arms hanging listlessly by their sides. I looked in vain for the monsters that inhabit those machines.

Suddenly, my eyes were attracted to the immense flock of black birds that hovered directly below me. They circled to the ground, and there before my eyes, stark and silent, lay the Martians, with the hungry birds pecking and tearing brown shreds of flesh from their dead bodies. Later when their bodies were examined in laboratories, it was found that they were killed by the putrefactive and disease bacteria against which their systems were unprepared . . . slain after all man's defenses had failed, by the humblest thing that God in His wisdom put upon this earth. . . .

Strange it now seems to sit in my peaceful study at Princeton writing down this last chapter of the record begun at a deserted farm at Grovers Mill. Strange to see from my window the university spires dim and blue through an April haze. Strange to watch children playing in the streets. Strange to see young people strolling on the green, where the new spring grass heals the last black scars of a bruised earth. Strange to watch the sightseers enter the museum where the dissembled parts of a Martian machine are kept on public view. Strange when I recall the time when I first saw it, bright and clean-cut, hard and silent, under the dawn of that last great day.

Writers as well as leading actors for the most popular serial of the decade, Freeman Gosden, left, played "Amos" to Charles Correll's "Andy."

Comics in "Black-Voice"

AMOS 'N' ANDY
MONDAY to FRIDAY, 7:00 E.S.T., NBC-*Red*

ANNOUNCER: **Here they are:—**

SYNOPSIS: **The Amos 'n' Andy** show was loaded with stereotyped black comedy roles —many of them played by Correll and Gosden—nearly as important as the title characters and just as popular with the audience. Two particular favorites were the Kingfish, top man in a fictitious Harlem lodge called the Mystic Knights of the Sea, and Lightnin', clean-up man of the lodge. As the sequence opens, the raffish Kingfish is practicing his customary wiles on the meek Lightnin'.

LIGHTNIN'
De fashion show was a financh success?

KINGFISH
Oh, yeh, it was great all right. Made close to a hundred dollars fo' de lodge, an' we is done paid our rent wid dat, an' light bill an' phone bill—all de utiliries.

LIGHTNIN'
Yessah—dat's good.

KINGFISH
Den it was voted last night to send some money oveh to de Harlem Boys' Club, oveh on 134th Street, on account o' de openin' today.

LIGHTNIN'
Yessah—dat's a big thing oveh dere fo' de chillun.

KINGFISH
Where's Amos 'n' Andy?

LIGHTNIN'
I seed Mr. Amos' taxicab, an' I was oveh talkin' to Mr. Andy dis mornin'—he was goin' home to bed. He didn't feel good.

KINGFISH
Too bad. Now, Lightnin', de reason I ast yo' to pay some o' yo' dues dat yo' is back in. De record show dat yo' ain't paid but thirty-five cents in de last two years, an' dat's a disregrace to de lodge dat's puttectin' yo' like it is.

LIGHTNIN'
Yessah, well, I is behind wid ev'rything; my coffin money's even back now. Insurance man come oveh dis mornin' lookin' fo' ten cents—I had to duck de man—I think dat's done lapsed on me.

KINGFISH
Wait a minute heah, don't fo'git dat dis lodge is givin' yo' puttection.

LIGHTNIN'
Well, I just ain't got it. If yo' would lend me some money, I would pay the lodge.

KINGFISH
Whut yo' mean, *me* lend yo' some money? I is flat as a pancake. I got about fifteen cents, an' I gotta git a dollar by tonight somewhere. We goin' have comp'ny fo' supper. De butcher done tighten up on me. I gotta git a couple o' po'k chops in dat house some way. Yo' can't ast de people comin' to supper to eat gravy *all* de time. . . .

LIGHTNIN'
Yessah.

KINGFISH
Can't you go to some friend?

LIGHTNIN'
I ain't got no money friends—all my friends is sympathy friends—dey listens an' feels sorry fo' me, but den dey's gone.

H. V. Kaltenborn stays with the microphone during a marathon newscast as assistants hand him the latest teletype reports of the Munich crisis.

War in Our Time

H. V. KALTENBORN
WEDNESDAY, 9:30 E.S.T. CBS

ANNOUNCER: H.V. Kaltenborn, dean of radio commentators . . . is going to tell you what he thinks about the headlines.

SYNOPSIS: On September 14, 1938, with the world watching hopefully, Britain's Prime Minister Chamberlain left London to negotiate with Chancellor Adolf Hitler over the German claims on Czechoslovakia. During the 18 days of the crisis, Kaltenborn was on call to make his comments—such as those below—on the fast-breaking news.

KALTENBORN

[Chamberlain] is risking his prestige, risking his position, risking almost everything upon this journey. And the amazing thing to me, is that he's risking it now, before things have actually come to the point where war does seem inevitable.

He has a plan—and perhaps that's the reason that he's going now. He has a plan that's been worked out between Britain and France. What can that plan be? Well, it can't be a plan for the immediate settlement of this problem. I don't believe that it would be possible to settle it as the result of a conversation between Chamberlain and Hitler alone. But, if the British follow the technique in which they are so adept and which they have used successfully in Spain and elsewhere, it will be a plan of postponement. The Czechoslovak delegate from Geneva said today: "Do we go on the butcher's block or have we found a champion who is going forth to battle?" Translated into other terms, that delegate is asking this: Must we Czechs give up to Germany our only dependable frontier, our richest industrial area and our right to exist as an independent nation? . . .

A great deal depends on the personal mood in which Hitler receives Chamberlain. Hitler is a man of moods. I've noticed that each time I've had personal contact with him. Berchtesgaden is one of the loveliest places in all the world. There Hitler has a beautiful Swiss chalet halfway up the green-covered mountainside, where he can stand and look into Austria. I was told that that was one reason why he chose it—because he could look across into his native Austria. I remember that when he invited me to Berchtesgaden he sent his private car with his chauffeur and the head of his Foreign Press service to Munich to meet me. I'm just wondering whether he's going to come to Munich himself to greet the Prime Minister of Britain.

If he does not, I think it will indicate he receives Chamberlain in the mood of a conqueror and that he considers that Chamberlain is coming to bargain. . . .

I am convinced that Chamberlain will not go away empty-handed. He is bound to get something. The Prime Minister of Britain who would visit the leader of Germany won't return completely empty-handed. Chamberlain is skillful enough, and the two men with him are sufficiently skillful in diplomacy, to bring back something. But my own feeling is that it will be little more than a truce. There is grave doubt as to whether or not the visit will bring peace.

Jack Benny's wife Mary, right, restrains Fred Allen and Fred's wife Portland, left, holds Jack back as the comedians act out their famous feud.

Jack's Face-off with Fred Allen

JELL-O PROGRAM
SUNDAY, 7:00 E.S.T., NBC-*Red*

ANNOUNCER: The Jell-O program, coming to you from the Grand Ballroom of the Hotel Pierre, starring Jack Benny, with Mary Livingstone, and Abe Lyman and his Orchestra.

SYNOPSIS: As part of his weekly routine, Jack has created a running feud with Fred Allen, star of Town Hall Tonight. But so far the two mock antagonists have never met. On this particular evening Jack opens the show with a series of anti-Allen jokes. Then he swings into a musical solo praising his own sponsor, Jell-O. He is interrupted by a loud knock on the door.

ALLEN
Whoever's blowing that foghorn . . . has gotta cut it out.

ALL
Fred Allen! *(Crowd: applause)*

BENNY
Well as I live and regret there are no locks on Studio doors . . . if it isn't [Fred] Allen!

. . . What's the idea of breaking in here in the middle of my singing?

ALLEN
Singing? When you set that croup to music and call it singing, you've gone too far!

BENNY
Now look here Allen, I don't care what you say about my singing on your *own* program, but after all, *I've* got listeners!

ALLEN
Keep your family out of this.

BENNY
Well my family likes my singing . . . and my violin playing, too.

ALLEN
Your violin playing! Why I just heard that a horse committed suicide when he found out your violin bow was made from his tail.

BENNY
Another crack like that and Town Hall will be looking for a new janitor.

ALLEN
You lay a hand on me and you'll be hollering Strawberry, Raspberry, Cherry, Orange, Lemon and *Help*.

BENNY
I'm a hard-ridin', two-fisted he-man . . . and if you'll step out in the hallway I'm ready to settle this little affair man to man!

MARY
Next week the Jell-O Program, starring Mary Livingstone! *(Jack and Fred exit, briefly. Then:)*

MARY
Sh, here they come now. *(Door opens, Jack and Allen enter—laughing)*

MARY
What happened to the fight?

JACK
What fight? . . .

ANNOUNCER DON WILSON
Hey fellows, what happened to that fight?

JACK
Why Don, we were never serious about that.

MARY
Then how did you get that black eye?

JACK
Oh, this? Well, I was writing a letter.

ALLEN
And I dotted his eye.

In a battle of quips, comedian W.C. Fields, right, and Charlie McCarthy, left, the dummy of ventriloquist Edgar Bergen, trade wooden glances.

Charlie McCarthy Meets His Match

CHASE & SANBORN HOUR
SUNDAY, 8:00 E.S.T., NBC-*Red*

ANNOUNCER: **The makers of Chase and Sanborn Coffee—the blend of the world's choice coffees—now being sold at a very reasonable price—present Constance Bennett, Dorothy Lamour, W.C. Fields, Edgar Bergen and Charlie McCarthy, Ray Middleton, Werner Janssen and Don Ameche!**

SYNOPSIS: **After chit-chat between actress Constance Bennett and Charlie, W.C. Fields, whom intimates called "Bill," is introduced by announcer Don Ameche. Then:**

BERGEN
Excuse me, Don. Am I intruding?

AMECHE
Frankly, Edgar, I'm glad you're here.

BERGEN
I hope I didn't interrupt anything. . . .

FIELDS
Not at all Edwin . . . not at all. . . .

BERGEN
Bill—I just came here to tell you something about Charlie.

FIELDS
I know enough about him already.

CHARLIE
Listen, Mr. Fields . . . I've got a bone to pick with you.

FIELDS
Yeah . . . Pick your head off.

CHARLIE
Aw gee whiz, Mr. Fields.

BERGEN
You've got Charlie all upset, Bill. He's tried all sorts of ways to make friends with you.

CHARLIE
Yes. I've had people intercede for me . . . I brought you a bouquet of flowers. . . .

FIELDS
A nosegay! Go on!

CHARLIE
I don't know where to go or what to do.

FIELDS
I can tell you where to go and also what to do. . . If you want me to go into details.

CHARLIE
I don't know . . . no matter what I say, it seems to be the wrong thing.

FIELDS
Then sew a button on your lip.

BERGEN
Now Bill . . . Charlie doesn't really feel good. Look how pale he is.

FIELDS
He needs a new coat of paint and a little furniture varnish.

CHARLIE
Mr. Fields, my mind is made up. I'm determined to fight fire with fire.

FIELDS
You know what happens to little boys who play with fire?

BERGEN
Don't mind Charlie, Bill. His bark is really worse than his bite.

FIELDS
I'll rip off his bark and bite off his limbs.

CHARLIE
This has gone far enough. I've been a little gentleman up to now. Mr. Fields . . . I'll clip you! So help me . . . I'll mow you down!

FIELDS
Go 'way—or I'll sic a woodpecker on you.

Breakfast with the Barbours

ONE MAN'S FAMILY
WEDNESDAY, 8:00 A.M. E.S.T., NBC-*Red*

ANNOUNCER: *One Man's Family* is dedicated to the Mothers and Fathers of the Younger Generation and to their Bewildering Offspring. Tonight we bring you Chapter Ten, Book Twenty-Three, entitled "Two Million Dollars At Stake." Philip Spencer was killed in a private plane crash, while en route to San Francisco to try to prove that he was the father of David, infant son of his ex-wife Beth Holly. Beth has declared that Spencer was *not* her child's father and was ready to go to any extreme to fight it. Now Spencer is gone and the danger is passed, but circumstances are not willing to let it go at that. *Now* the attorneys for Spencer's estate announce that the deceased has left funds and property to the value of two million dollars; that the only known possible heir is the baby David; and that he will inherit the full amount *providing* Beth can prove that David is Spencer's child. And while Beth faces this new dilemma, Clifford and Ann are walking on air. Father and Mother Barbour have given them a round-trip ticket from San Francisco to Hong Kong on the China Clipper for their honeymoon! This happened last night at the engagement shower for the couple . . . and now the family is at breakfast. . . .

FANNY
(*Coming to Mike*) Now Clifford, eat your breakfast like a normal human being. . . .

CLIFF
But Mom, Dad says the Clipper Ship crosses the Equator on the way to Hong Kong, and it doesn't at all.

HENRY
Certainly you cross the Equator. . . .

CLIFF
No Dad—

FANNY
Are you going to eat your bacon and eggs?

CLAUDIA
What's bacon and eggs in Cliff's young life?

FANNY
Well if I'd known what a goose he was going to be, I'd have put my foot down when your father wanted to buy the tickets. . . .

HAZEL
He hasn't talked about anything else. . . .

CLIFF
But you folks don't *get* it . . . Ann and I are going to *fly the Pacific Ocean* . . . (*Laughter*)

JACK
(*Bored*) Sure we got it . . . You're going to *fly the Pacific* (*Laughter*)

FANNY
Clifford, where are you going?

CLIFF
(*Leaving Mike*) I just want to get the globe.

CLAUDIA
(*Laughs*) Crazy as a loon.

FANNY
Such a business. He's more excited about that trip than about getting married.

HAZEL
(*Amused*) They both are. Ann was so excited before she left last night she was ill. . . .

HENRY
Well their excitement is infectious. . . . I don't know when I've enjoyed giving a present so much. . . .

FANNY
Well it should have worn off a little by this morning. . . . I'm going to be worn to a frazzle if this hilarity keeps up. . . .

CLIFF
(*Coming to Mike*) Here you are Dad. It's just as I said. We don't cross the Equator.

FANNY
Clifford, your breakfast is stone cold. . . .

CLIFF
You see, this is Midway and this is Wake.

FANNY
Humph. . . . Look like fly-specks to *me*. . . . (*Laughter*)

In "One Man's Family," Minetta Ellen, far left, played Fanny (Mother Barbour); and J. Anthony Smythe, far right, was Henry (Father Barbour).

Hard Times

Shacks of Seattle's Hooverville shelter the homeless.

The Hungry Years

I remember lying in bed one night and thinking. All at once I realized something. We were poor. Lord! It was weeks before I could get over that.

DEPRESSION VICTIM, CHATTANOOGA, TENNESSEE, 1933

In 1930, before the full effect of the Depression was felt across the country, most Americans knew poverty only by reputation. But in the next several years, a large part of the richest nation on earth learned what it meant to be poor; for 40 million people poverty became a way of life.

Misery found its way into every region, group and occupation. Black factory workers, always the last to be hired in good times, were the first to be fired as production slowed to a painful crawl. Farmers, struggling to keep on their feet amid plummeting crop prices, were knocked down for good by a series of natural disasters—floods, droughts, plagues and dust storms. Businessmen slipped from being home owners to room renters, and even to wandering the street. Experience taught many children to move their dolls about in a game they called Eviction.

"The Depression had pups on our doorstep." So said an Oklahoma farmer whose ill-fortune had multiplied, though he was lucky enough to keep his doorstep. But the luckless were legion, homeless and on the move. Foreclosed farmers became migratory field hands in the West. Sharecroppers drifted north, plodding from city to city in search of a job and a breadline. Ragged bands of youths roamed the country aimlessly, sleeping in hobo jungles.

Naturally, all these wanderers suffered poignantly from cold, hunger and disease. Not so naturally, many were denied relief because they had no legal residence.

Even those fortunate Americans who managed to live out the decade in well-heeled comfort were often shaken by the misery they saw or read about. One *had* to wince at the courage of an Arkansas family that walked 900 miles to apply for work; and then wince again at the bitter humor of a penniless Southerner who announced, "When you gits down to your last bean, your backbone and your navel shakes dice to see which gits it." It was easy to cry at the sacrifice offered by a destitute mother who, after giving birth to her seventh child, told the doctor, "I've never been able to pay you nothin' for deliverin' my other six children; so I'll give you this one."

By 1939, the worst was over; the Depression had made a hero of every sufferer who managed to survive. The names of the poor were largely lost to posterity. But the experience that scourged them survived, recorded with heartbreaking fidelity by photographers, reporters and social workers. The words and pictures gathered by these chroniclers did more than capture the raw emotions of the moment. They captured the soul of the Depression.

Competition was stiff among the apple sellers in New York. Said one peddler, "People mostly hurry by as if they didn't want to look at you."

The Face of Poverty

Before daylight we were on the way to Chevrolet. The police were
already on the job, waving us away from the office.
"Nothin' doin'. Nothin' doin'." Now we were tramping through
falling snow. Dodge employment office. A big
well fed man in a heavy overcoat stood at the door saying, "No, no,"
as we passed before him. On the tramp again. . . .

AN UNEMPLOYED DETROIT AUTO WORKER

Desperate for work, a Detroiter advertises. Others bought jobs; one man paid a $10 fee to earn $13.50.

Jobless New Yorkers haunt the employment agencies on Sixth Avenue. One agency averaged 5,000 applicants daily—and had work for only 300.

A toil-worn California field hand faces an uncertain future. "I have worked hard all my life," said one man, "and all I have now is my broken body."

We had been eating wild greens since January
this year. Violet tops, wild onions, forget-me-not, wild lettuce
and such weeds as cows eat. Our family are in bad
shape childrens need milk women need nurishments food shoes
and dresses—that we cannot get.
A KENTUCKY MINER

A tubercular New York mother still believed she could make it: "Long as I can work, I'll get along somehow."

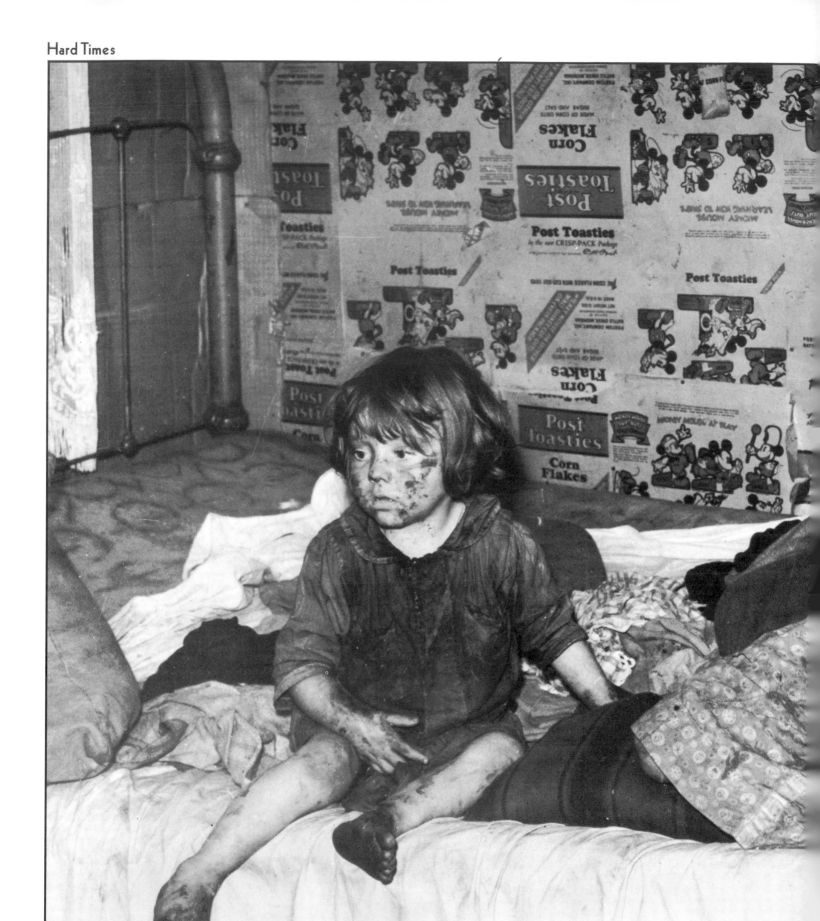

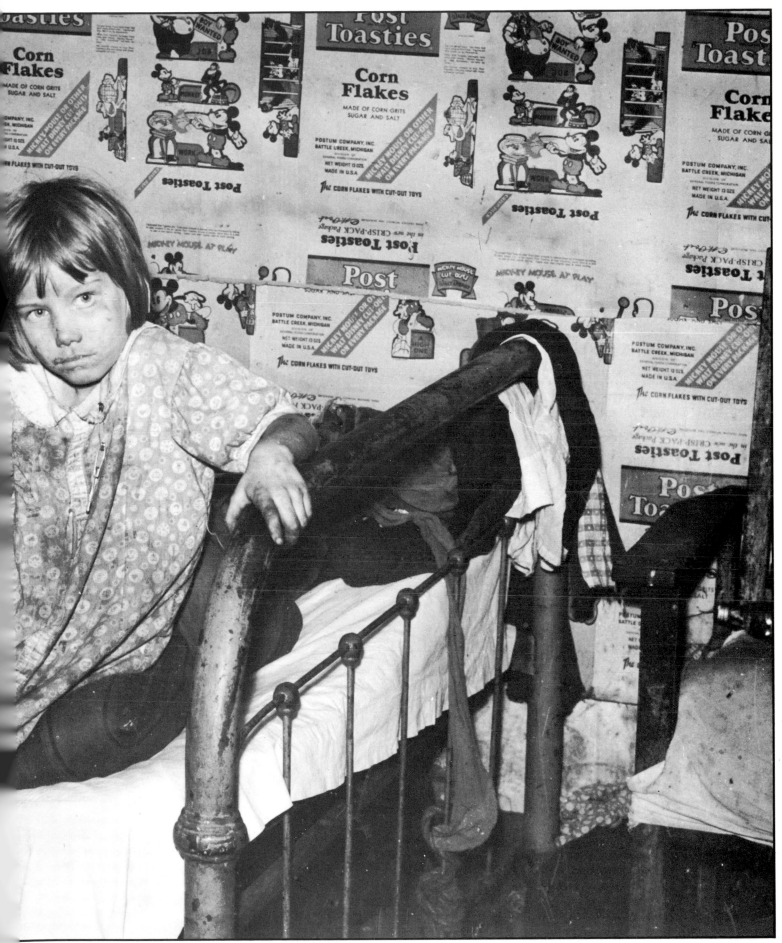

The daughters of a WPA worker and a sick mother are left home unattended. A bitter father said: "A worker's got no right to have kids any more."

Ragged but tough, a South Carolina farm girl remains unintimidated. Many such children worked in the fields from "can see" to "can't see."

*If they come to take my farm, I'm going to fight. I'd rather be
killed outright than die by starvation. But before I die, I'm going to set fire
to my crops, I'm going to burn my house, I'm going to p'izen my cattle.*
A DEBT-RIDDEN FARMER

Destitute but steadfast, a miner's family keeps up its spirits during the bitter 1939 strike in the coal fields of West Virginia.

Adding to the burden of the Depression, the Ohio River invades Louisville in 1937. In that year of high water, a million people needed flood relief.

The Hand of Nature

Oh, I tell you I've seen that old river come up.
When it begins to git in the houses,
we take and move everything up on the bank
across the railroad tracks.
Well, city folks come trotting up there with soup
kettles. They's always one saying to
another, "Do you suppose them people's got little
enough sense to go back to them
shacks when the river goes down?" Yes Lord,
we'll always go back to Shanty Town
till the river rises some day and forgits to go down.
A TENNESSEE SQUATTER

The receding flood water leaves mud and wreckage inside an Indiana farmhouse.

Flood victims line up for food and pure water. Said a relief worker: "It ain't going to hurt the government to feed and clothe them that needs it."

After years of drought, the great dust storm of May 21, 1937, strikes Clayton, New Mexico. Despite dust masks, many died of suffocation.

*When these winds hit us, we and
our misery were suddenly covered with dust.
Here in the Texas Panhandle
we were hit harder than most anywhere
else. If the wind blew one way,
here came the dark dust from Oklahoma.
Another way and it was the gray
dust from Kansas. Still another way, the
brown dust from Colorado and
New Mexico. Little farms were buried. And
the towns were blackened.*

A TEXAS FARMER

*These storms were like rolling black
smoke. We had to keep the lights on all day.
We went to school with headlights on,
and with dust masks on. I saw a woman who
thought the world was coming
to an end. She dropped down on her knees in
the middle of Main Street in
Amarillo and prayed out loud: "Dear Lord!
Please give them another chance."*

A TEXAS SCHOOLBOY

An abandoned farm lies inundated by dust. Departing farmers reduced the population of Hall County, Texas, from 14,392 to only 7,000.

All that dust made some of the
farmers leave; they became the Okies. We stuck
it out here. We scratched, literally
scratched, to live. We'd come to town to sell
sour cream for nine cents
a pound. If we could find a town big
enough and far enough away
from the dust, we could sell eggs at ten cents
a dozen. Despite all the dust
and the wind, we were putting in crops, but
making no crops and barely
living out of barnyard products only. We
made five crop failures in five years.

AN OKLAHOMA FARMER

"For Sale" signs marked the start of the dust bowlers' migrations.

Heading west, migrants gaze wearily from their car. For them, California, the "Land of Milk and Honey," would offer drudgery and privation.

The Promise of the Road

This is a hard life to swallow, but I just couldn't sit
back there and look to someone to feed us.
A MIGRATORY WORKER

A hapless Okie grimly looks across the desert: "Yessir, we're starved, stalled and stranded."

Too poor to ride, a family from Arkansas walks through Texas to look for work in the Rio Grande cotton fields, a trek of about 900 miles.

October-December 1932. Cut Malaga and muscat grapes

near Fresno. About $40 a month.

December 1932. Left for Imperial Valley, Calif.

February 1933. Picked peas, Imperial Valley. Earned $30 for season.

On account of weather, was fortunate to break even.

March-April 1933. Left for Chicago. Returned to California.

May 1933. Odd jobs on lawns and radios at Fresno.

June 1933. Picked figs near Fresno. Earned $50 in two months.

A MIGRATORY WORKER'S LOG BOOK

Rude cardboard shacks served as winter quarters for migrants in California's Imperial Valley.

A large family, intact despite its migrations, gathers to share a simple meal. "Us people has got to stick together to get by these hard times."

A Tennessee woman succumbs to despondency: "I've wrote back that we're well and such as that, but I never have wrote that we live in a tent."

We make as much as is fitten for such as us runnin'-around

folks. Caint send the children to school we aint got the clothes. By a'savin up we get

so's we can move on to the next place. We haven't had no help no way.

A TEXAS MIGRANT IN CALIFORNIA

When they need us they call us migrants.

When we've picked their crops we're bums and we've got to get out.

A MIGRATORY WORKER

A worker improvises his morning shave. In some camps shaving was a luxury: "You can't waste water when it costs so much to get."

Successful in California, a migrant's wife admires their farm. Said she proudly: "One more piece of pipe and our water tank will be finished."

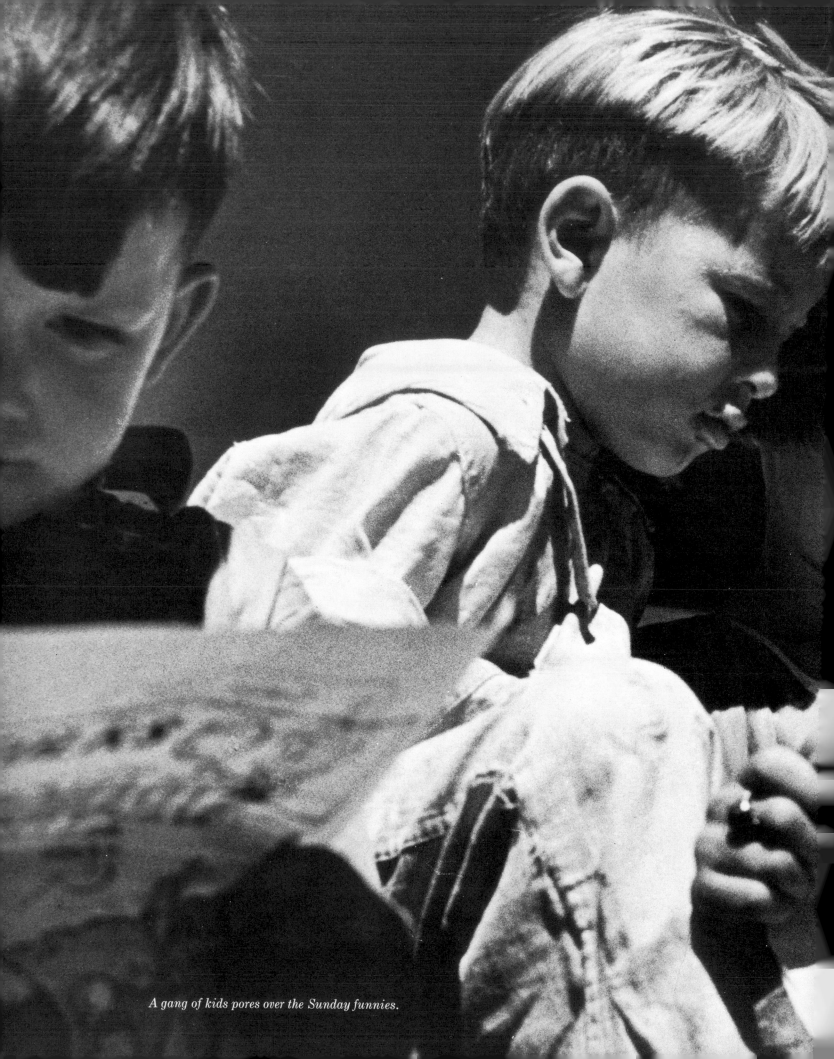

A gang of kids pores over the Sunday funnies.

The Company of Heroes

Leapin' Lizards! Who says business is bad?

During the '30s, the world of little kids orbited around a set of heroes and heroines whose extravagant lives were chronicled in a rich new range of media. Every Sunday before church, kids all over the country pawed through the funny papers for the latest exploits of Flash Gordon or Little Orphan Annie, whose pet expression "Leapin' Lizards!" was an American standard and whose faith in good old capitalism comforted many a Depression-ridden parent. On weekdays Annie also came booming over the radio, joined by the likes of hard-bitten detective Dick Tracy and Jack Armstrong, a teen-age football hero. Saturday was movie day: four and a half raucous hours of cliff-hanging serials featuring Tarzan or Flash Gordon, animated cartoons, and then perhaps a full-length picture starring that all-time heroine, Shirley Temple. In between times, the kids caught up on back adventures of the same characters through Big Little Books—squat, 400-page cubes of type and pictures that sold for a dime—or amused themselves with pop-up and cut-out books of Shirley, Buck Rogers or a pair of overseas idols, Princesses Elizabeth and Margaret Rose of England.

The kingdoms of these heroes and heroines were even more varied than the media that brought them home to the kids; they ranged from America's playing fields to the slimiest Oriental jungles, from the plains of the Old West to the slums of gangster-ridden cities, from Buckingham Palace to galaxies in the far reaches of outer space. And the idols themselves were just as varied in their makeup; some were real (the Little Princesses), some wholly fabricated (Buck Rogers), others physically real but fictitious in their exploits (Tom Mix and Shirley Temple).

The common ground on which these heroes and heroines stood was virtue, a commodity they sold in heaping portions by proving that good, clean living held unlimited rewards. With the exception of the Little Princesses, the idols also proved awesomely adept at selling commercial products. With each installment of their adventures, they unblushingly fired off a barrage of sales pitches in behalf of various trinkets, toys and breakfast foods. Little Orphan Annie even managed to pitch a chocolate drink called Ovaltine with her left hand while handing out her conservative, pro-business dogma with the right. Despite such blatant salesmanship, however, the most successful product served up by the kids' idols was an inexpensive and wonderful world of make-believe, during hard times when the real world often seemed to be no fun at all.

Moppets, carefully coiffed and rehearsed by would-be movie mothers, participate in a Shirley Temple look-alike contest in Herrin, Illinois.

When Little Orphan Annie first appeared, she seemed out of place on the funny pages, for the simple reason that she was rarely funny. Rather, cartoonist Harold Gray time and again rallied his never-aging red-haired tyke and her mongrel Sandy to the aid of decent folks who were cowering before treacherous foreigners, mortgage-holders and crimelords. Often Annie's wealthy foster father, Oliver "Daddy" Warbucks, would happen by with his homicidal henchmen Punjab and The Asp to give Annie a hand.

Launched in 1924, the strip's success soon affected *Annie's* story line. Gray, who by 1934 was earning about $100,000 a year, began to color the melodrama with his conservative views on labor leaders and liberal politicians. Only when Annie went on radio did Gray compromise his —and the orphan's—philosophy of "ya hafta earn what ya get"; Annie gave away a glittering array of premiums in exchange for seals from the jars of sponsor Ovaltine's chocolate milk mix. However, $1,000 a week soothed Gray's anguish at the thought of all those free rings, badges, shake-up mugs and those secret-code cards *(right)* that allowed Annie's radio followers to decode such momentous messages as: 8-36-18-28-22/30-44-2-24-40-18-28-10.

ANNIE RINGS

BUTTONS

SHAKE-UP MUG

SECRET SOCIETY BADGES AND CODE

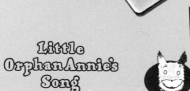

Little Orphan Annie's Song

BRACELETS

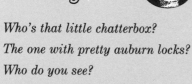

Who's that little chatterbox?
The one with pretty auburn locks?
Who do you see?
It's Little Orphan Annie. . . .

Bright eyes, cheeks a rosy glow,
There's a store of healthiness handy.
Mite-size, always on the go.
And if you want to know—"Arf!" says Sandy. . . .

FLASH GORDON

When the planet Mongo threatened to collide with Earth in 1934, Yale-bred polo player Flash Gordon and a beautiful girl named Dale Arden were kidnaped aboard the rocket of crazed genius Hans Zarkov. With that notion for openers, cartoonist Alex Raymond launched the Flash Gordon story, first on the comic pages and eventually on the screen and in Big Little Books.

Guided by Raymond's fertile imagination, Flash, Dale and Dr. Zarkov journeyed from Earth to Mongo; during the trip Zarkov miraculously regained his sanity, having first calculated that the runaway planet would miss

Earth. Though the folks at home were now presumably safe, Flash and his friends were not, for Mongo was ruled by yellow-skinned, almond-eyed Ming the Merciless, who was evil incarnate in the 1930s, when Americans were fretting increasingly over the Yellow Peril of emerging Asia. On Mongo, Flash was ever the target of sensual women and unspeakably foul agents of the wily Ming. Yet he remained true both to Dale and the values of the Yale polo field (as interpreted by Raymond): "This was a Tournament of Death, but it was still to be fought by heroes imbued with the ideals of sportsmanship and fair play."

In films, Olympic swim star Buster Crabbe played a peroxided Flash.

PEDOMETER

HOVERING DISCS AND GUN

Jack Armstrong!

"The All-American Boy!!" As the radio announcer shouted those magic words and a male chorus swung into the "Hudson High Fight Song," millions of kids began to live through the latest adventure of brainy, brawny, awesomely pure-in-heart Jack Armstrong. The All-American Boy's missions were three: to lead Hudson High to athletic glory, to overcome all bad guys and to peddle Wheaties. Naturally Jack broke all scoring records for Hudson High and for Wheaties, in whose behalf he unloaded tons of crispy wheat flakes and scads of premiums. At the same time the show served up heaping portions of fair play and love for America, the latter being shoe-horned into every possible line of script—as witness the dialogue below.

Tell the boys and girls of the United States this world is theirs. If they have hearts of gold, a glorious new golden age awaits us. If they are honest, riches shall be theirs. If they are kind, they shall save the whole world from malice and meanness. Will you take that message to the boys and girls of the United States, Jack Armstrong?

TIBETAN MONK TO JACK ARMSTRONG, 1939.

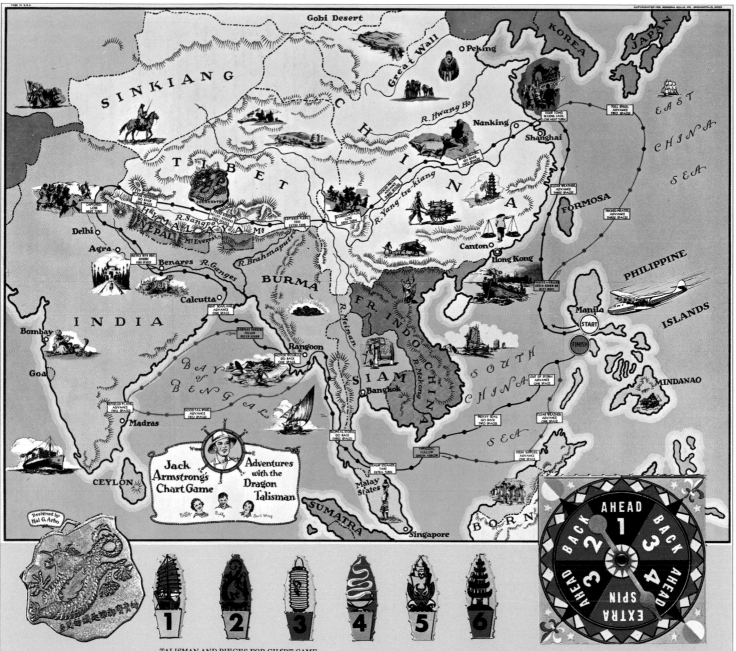

Jack Armstrong's Chart Game

Adventures with the Dragon Talisman

Designed by Hal G. Arbo

TALISMAN AND PIECES FOR CHART GAME

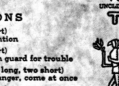

THE WHEATIES SONG

Won't you try Wheaties?

They're whole wheat with all of the bran.

Won't you try Wheaties?

For wheat is the best food of man.

HUDSON HIGH FIGHT SONG

Wave the flag for Hudson High, boys,

Show them how we stand!

Ever shall our team be champions,

Known throughout the land!

Rah Rah Boola Boola Boola Boola.

WHISTLE RING

JACK ARMSTRONG'S
SECRET WHISTLE CODE

JACK ARMSTRONG

UNCLE JIM

INSTRUCTIONS

One Whistle	(Short) Attention
Two Whistles	(Short) Be on guard for trouble
Three Whistles	(One long, two short) In danger, come at once
Four Whistles	(Short) We're being watched
Two Whistles	(Two Long) Important news — meet me at once

BETTY

BILLY

Tarzan

In 1914 a middle-aged hack writer named Edgar Rice Burroughs collected rejection slips from every major American publisher before he finally sold his first novel: *Tarzan of the Apes*. This bizarre adventure story, set in the jungles of darkest Africa, told of the nurturing of an orphaned year-old boy, scion of the English House of Greystoke, by a fierce she-ape named Kala. In Kala's warm embrace, both Tarzan ("White Skin" in ape language) and Edgar Rice Burroughs grew and prospered.

By the end of the 1930s, Tarzan was the established hero of 21 fast-selling novels, a deftly drawn comic strip

(above), a 15-minute daily radio serial and 16 movies. Most popular with Tarzan fans in this decade were the movies, with their "take-me-to-the-elephant-graveyard" plots and their deathless dialogue, the best of it uttered by Olympic swim star Johnny Weissmuller during his incumbency in the title role. In his first film, *Tarzan, the Ape Man (right)*, Weissmuller enlarged the American vocabulary with the line "Me Tarzan, you Jane" and also introduced his fearful jungle yodel, a mixture of five sounds that included his own scream, a soprano singing high C and a recording of a hyena's howl played backwards.

1. In an early scene in "Tarzan, the Ape Man," ivory-hunters James Parker and Harry Holt quiz natives about the elephant graveyard.

2. The safari, including Maureen O'Sullivan as Parker's daughter Jane, hears an unearthly cry and finds its path blocked by Tarzan.

3. Infatuated by Jane, Tarzan kidnaps her. At first, she balks at sharing Tarzan's treehouse with either the Ape Man or his chum Cheeta.

4. Jane falls in love with Tarzan and teaches him to speak. During a lakeside frolic, he utters the immortal "Me Tarzan, you Jane."

5. Conscience-smitten, Jane returns to her father as the safari is captured by Pygmies; Tarzan and his jungle pals swing to the rescue.

FADEOUT: The safari over, Jane decides to become the mate of Tarzan, who takes her to the mountain for a view of her new jungle domain.

COMIC BOOK PREMIUM

MEMBERSHIP OATH

MEMBERSHIP SONG

AUTOGRAPHED PHOTO OF TONY AND TOM

Tom Mix

"Reach for the sky! Lawbreakers always lose, Straight Shooters always win!! It pays to shoot straight!!!" Young radio listeners thrilled to hear cowboy character Tom Mix bark out this instructive battle cry. Naturally, when their hero commanded them to eat his sponsor Ralston's wheat cereal, they hastened to do so; and when Tom said that a few Ralston box tops would yield the treasures shown here, what real Straight Shooter could resist?

Tom's radio fans had plenty of company in their worship of the hard-jawed idol. Long before the radio show began in 1933, Mix had built up an international following that had rooted for him and the Wonder Horse Tony through some 180 feature films.

In real life, the old Straight Shooter was an old roué who ran through three wives and four million dollars. Nevertheless he guarded his public image as a nonsmoking teetotaler. "I want to keep my pictures in such a vein that parents will not object to letting their children see me on the screen," explained Tom solemnly. And all his fans believed him, remaining loyal literally to the end: when he died in 1940, the Tom Mix Club of Lisbon, Portugal, gave up movies for two weeks as a sign of mourning.

SLIDE-WHISTLE RING

SIGNATURE RING

COMPASS AND MAGNIFIER

CLUB BADGE

SIREN RING

MAGNET RING

MIRROR RING

CLUB RING

HORSESHOE NAIL RING

WRANGLER BADGE

DECODER BADGE

COWBOY SPUR

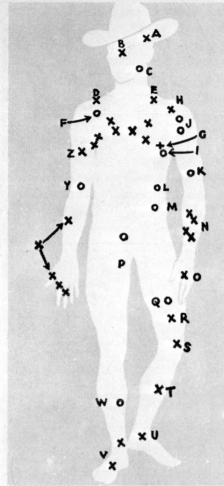

TOM MIX' INJURIES

Danger and difficulty have never daunted Tom Mix, nor broken bones stopped him. He has been blown up once, shot 12 times and injured 47 times in movie stunting. The chart shows the location of some of Tom's injuries. (X marks fractures; circles, bullet wounds.)

A. Skull fractured in accident.
B. Nose injured when artillery wagon blew up in China.
C. Shot thru jaw by sniper in Spanish-American War.
D. Shoulder fractured in circus accident.
E. Collar bone broken four times in falls.
F. Shot by bandit in Mix home.
G. Eight broken ribs from movie accidents.
H. Shoulder fractured when horse was shot from under him by bandits in U. S. Marshal days.
I. Shot by cattle rustlers in Texas.
J. Shot twice in left arm by Oklahoma outlaws.
K. Shot below elbow by outlaw.
L. Shot through abdomen by killer he arrested.
M. Wounded in gun fight with rustlers.
N. Left arm broken four times in movie stunting.
O. Hand broken in movie stunt.
P. Shot by bad man while Oklahoma sheriff.
Q. Shot in leg when 14 years old.
R. Leg trampled by horse.
S. Fractured knee in wagon accident.
T. Leg broken while stunting for movies.
U. Fractured ankle breaking wild horses.
V. Foot and ankle broken in wagon accident.
W. Shot through leg by bank robbers.
X. Three broken fingers, hand and arm fractured in screen fights and film stunting.
Y. Shot through elbow in real stage coach hold-up (1902).
Z. Broken arm in film stunting.

NOTE: *Scars from twenty-two knife wounds are not indicated, nor is it possible to show on the diagram the hole four inches square and many inches deep that was blown in Tom's back by a dynamite explosion.*

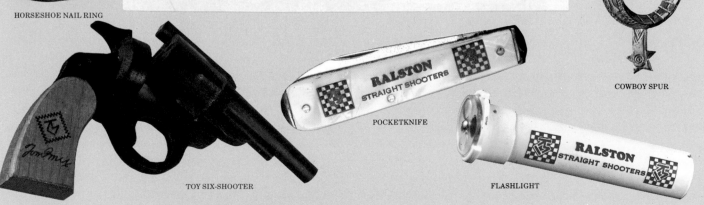
TOY SIX-SHOOTER

POCKETKNIFE

FLASHLIGHT

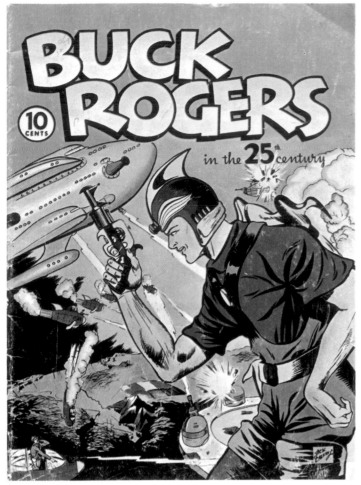

COMIC BOOKS

BUCK ROGERS POCKET WATCH

SOLAR SCOUTS BADGE

"Wilma, does all your equipment check out?" "Yes, Buck, I have my Thermic Radiation Projector, the Electro-cosmic Spectrometer and the Super Radiating Protono-former all set to go!" And so Buck Rogers and his luscious co-pilot Wilma Deering blasted off through the comics and radio on another mission to save "the whole universe."

All of Buck's adventures were marked by this same wild conglomeration of technological prophecy and sheer driv-el, and the climax of each plot was woefully predictable: Buck would capture archvillains Killer Kane and the slinky Ardala and commit them to the intergalactic Re-habilitation Center—from which they invariably escaped.

Killer and Ardala should have stayed put, for they were up against the combined brains and muscle of the Solar Scouts plus an ingenious arsenal of cosmic weapons that included Rocket Pistols, whose discharge introduced to the language the death-sound ZAP, and Atomic Bombs. These weapons of the future were fascinating to Buck's 20th Century fans; when Macy's department store in New York advertised it had toy versions of Buck Rogers Disin-tegrator Guns, the next morning a queue of 20,000 peo-ple—a third-of-a-mile-long—awaited the store's opening.

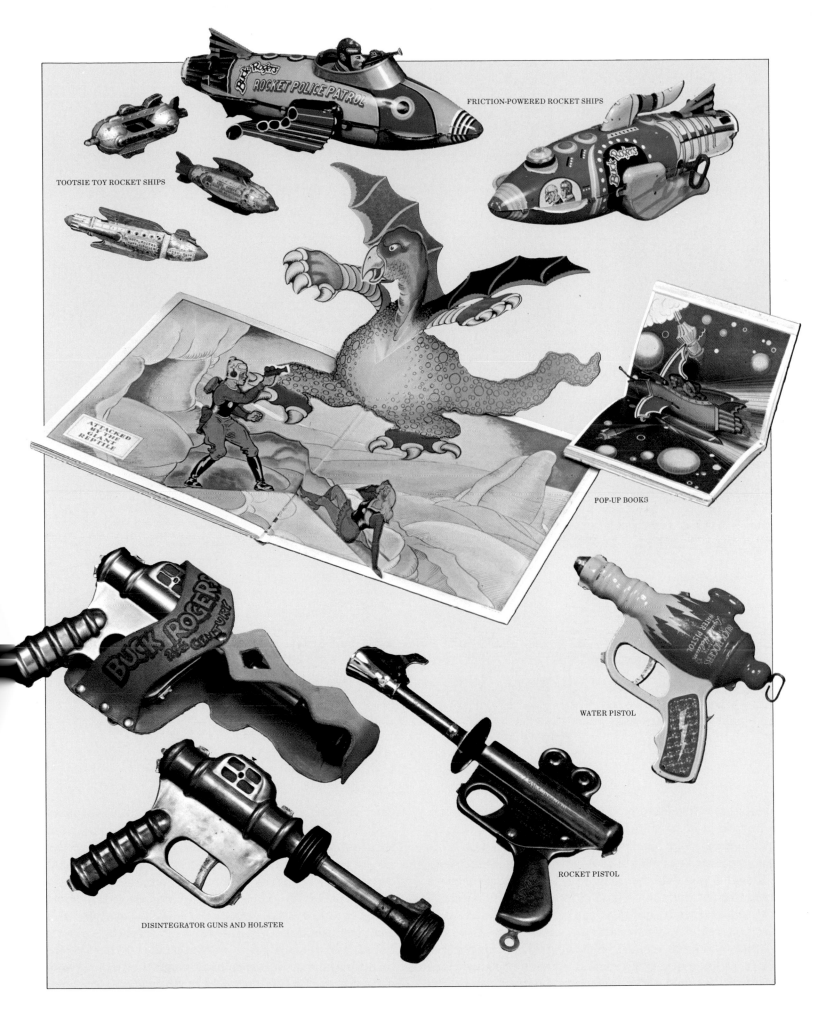

FRICTION-POWERED ROCKET SHIPS

TOOTSIE TOY ROCKET SHIPS

POP-UP BOOKS

WATER PISTOL

DISINTEGRATOR GUNS AND HOLSTER

ROCKET PISTOL

DETECTIVE BADGE

ROOKIE BADGE

SOPHOMORE BADGE

CLUB BUTTON

OFFICIAL WATCH

SERGEANT

SECRET SERVICE PATROL OFFICER BADGES

LIEUTENANT

CAPTAIN

DICK TRACY

Dick Tracy, the sharp-profiled comic strip detective, was a natural product of the '30s. Describing his cartoon creation, artist Chester Gould said, "Big gangsters were running wild but going to court and getting off scot free. I thought: why not have a guy who doesn't take the gangsters to court but shoots 'em?" So saying, Gould launched a strip loaded with gunfire. In the very first week, the slaying of Jeremiah Trueheart (right) marked the first time anyone had been gunned to death on the funny pages. More, much more, was to follow, for Dick Tracy, fiancé of Trueheart's daughter Tess, was so moved by this foul

deed that he signed on for life with the police force.

Quaker Oats cereal brought the detective to radio and soon devised a diabolically cunning sales gimmick: the Dick Tracy Secret Service Patrol. A boy's rise up the patrol hierarchy was directly proportional to how much Quaker Oats he could cram down, for a sergeant's badge cost five boxtops, a lieutenant's, seven, and so on. The company mercifully stopped the escalation at 15 box tops, but added a fillip for cereal-swelled candidates bucking for the ultimate rank of Inspector-General: they had to come up with a new Quaker Oats-gobbling recruit for the patrol.

Panels selected from the first two weeks of strips show how Dick Tracy's jaw began to jut dangerously after thugs slew his fiancée's father.

ELIZABETH   MARGARET ROSE

The Little Princesses

On the morning of May 12, 1937, two pretty, curly-haired little girls in purple robes and golden coronets stood on a balcony alongside their parents and waved at a cheering throng. On that day Elizabeth and Margaret Rose Windsor of Great Britain (*above*) fulfilled a dream cherished by just about every little girl in the Western world: their daddy was crowned King—of England, no less—and they were going to live in a real palace.

Eleven-year-old Princess Elizabeth and six-year-old Princess Margaret Rose quickly became international heroines and the subjects of a batch of hastily assembled biographies, story books (including one told from the viewpoint of their pet dogs) and paper-doll books. With the latter, a little girl anywhere could cut out dresses, fold the tabs over punch-out figures (*left*) and together with her own two princess pals, dream through a delicious range of royal fantasies, including a private coronation.

SHIRLEY TEMPLE

"My first impression of Shirley was a bit of sunshine. She had on a yellow dress and yellow coat and all that golden hair." This loving commentary by Shirley Temple's studio schoolteacher summed up the doting affection of the whole nation for the blonde moppet who swiftly became the child of the decade after she sang and danced, at the age of 5, in the 1934 movie *Stand Up and Cheer*.

In one of the many films that followed, Shirley was "Little Miss Marker"; she might well have been called "Little Miss Mark-Up" in real life. As Hollywood's top box-office draw from 1935 to 1938, her average of four pictures a year grossed five million dollars annually and was credited with keeping her studio solvent. Miss Temple's yearly $300,000 salary was boosted by royalties from a swarm of merchandisers of Shirley-endorsed dolls, doll clothes and accessories, soap, books and ribbons. Her doll manufacturer alone sold some six million toy moppets—at $3 to $30 each—in boxes bearing the star's own childish scrawl *(above)*. Outfits for these dolls *(overleaf)* often cost more than dresses for real girls. Even hairdressers profited from the star's popularity; they were besieged by girls demanding golden, 56-curled hairdos, just like Shirley's.

Shirley Temple Doll owners were deluged with dresses inspired by the star's movie roles.

Cops and Robbers

The wages of crime for Bonnie and Clyde is death in this bullet-ridden auto.

The Daredevil Crooks

The criminal army in America today is on the march. . . . Crime is today sapping the spiritual and moral strength of America.

J. EDGAR HOOVER

Johnnie's just an ordinary fellow. Of course, he goes out and holds up banks and things, but he's really just like any other fellow, aside from that.

A FRIEND OF JOHN DILLINGER

Hard times brought a marked boom for at least one profession—crime. While legitimate businesses closed and farms lay barren, an alarming number of Americans began looking for easy money through robbery, kidnaping and even murder. Across the Midwest, bands of marauders traveling in fast-moving cars and toting sawed-off shotguns and Tommy guns began knocking over rural banks and Post Offices. In large cities, tightly organized undergrounds were raking in millions of dollars through extortion, prostitution and auto theft rings. By 1935, according to one estimate by the Justice Department, so many Americans had moved to the shady side of the law that crooks outnumbered carpenters by four to one, grocers by six to one and doctors by 20 to one.

The first of the decade's lawbreakers to win real notoriety, and surely the most hated criminal of his time, was an ex-convict from Germany named Bruno Richard Hauptmann. On the night of March 1, 1932, Hauptmann climbed up to a second-story nursery bedroom in Hopewell, New Jersey, and kidnaped the 20-month-old son of aviation hero Charles Lindbergh. The nation was stunned. It was as though Hauptmann had violated every home in America. For Lindy was the country's favorite hero, a modest, tousled-haired symbol of American courage and integrity. Though Lindy paid $50,000 in ransom, the baby was found dead six weeks later, and when Hauptmann was finally caught and executed in the electric chair, the country registered deep satisfaction.

But the country had some strikingly different feelings about other crimes and criminals; many people, impoverished and embittered by the Depression, actually found a certain justice in the mounting number of bank robberies. The most notorious of the bank thieves, John Dillinger, even emerged as a kind of Robin Hood folk hero. "Dillinger did not rob poor people. He robbed those who became rich by robbing the poor," wrote an admirer in Indianapolis. "I am for Johnnie." Indeed, Dillinger projected an image of swashbuckling glamor and generosity. When holding up a bank he would leap the barrier to the teller's cage to grab the loot. Once, when he broke out with two hostages from a supposedly escape-proof Indiana jail, he gave the men four dollars carfare home. In their admiration Dillinger's fans managed to forget that their hero had gunned down 10 men during his career, and that—like the other bandits shown on the following pages—he was basically just a cold-blooded thug.

America's No. 1 desperado, John Dillinger, smiles while he shows off some of the tools of his trade: a Thompson submachine gun and a pistol.

GET·DILLINGER!
$15,000 Reward
A PROCLAMATION

WHEREAS, One John Dillinger stands charged officially with numerous felonies including murder in several states and his banditry and depredation stamp him as an outlaw, a fugitive from justice and a vicious menace to life and property;

NOW, THEREFORE, We, Paul McNutt, Governor of Indiana; George White, Governor of Ohio; F. B. Olson, Governor of Minnesota; William A. Comstock, Governor of Michigan; and Henry Horner, Governor of Illinois, do hereby proclaim and offer a reward of Five Thousand Dollars ($5,000.00) to be paid to the person or persons who apprehend and deliver the said John Dillinger into the custody of any sheriff of any of the above-mentioned states or his duly authorized agent.

THIS IS IN ADDITION TO THE $10,000.00 OFFERED BY THE FEDERAL GOVERNMENT FOR THE ARREST OF JOHN DILLINGER.

HERE IS HIS FINGERPRINT CLASSIFICATION and DESCRIPTION. ——— FILE THIS FOR IDENTIFICATION PURPOSES.

John Dillinger, (w) age 30 yrs., 5-8½, 160½ lbs., gray eyes, med. chest, hair, med. comp., med. build. Dayton, O., P. D. No. 10587. O. S. B. No. 559-646.

F.P.C. (12)

$$\frac{M \quad 9 \quad R \quad O \quad O}{S \quad 14 \quad U \quad OO \quad 8}$$

13 10 OO O O
u R w w w
5 11 15 I 8
u U u w u

FRONT VIEW

Be on the lookout for this desperado. He is heavily armed and usually is protected with bullet-proof vest. Take no unnecessary chances in getting this man. He is thoroughly prepared to shoot his way out of any situation.

GET HIM

DEAD
OR ALIVE

Notify any Sheriff or Chief of Police of Indiana, Ohio, Minnesota, Michigan, Illinois.

or **THIS BUREAU**

SIDE VIEW

ILLINOIS STATE BUREAU OF CRIMINAL IDENTIFICATION AND INVESTIGATION
J. P. Sullivan, Supt. Springfield, Illinois

Wanted for murder, robbery and half a dozen other felonies, Dillinger grew a moustache and altered his fingerprints with acid to escape detection.

WANTED

LESTER M. GILLIS,

aliases GEORGE NELSON, "BABY FACE" NELSON, ALEX GILLIS, LESTER GILES,

"BIG GEORGE" NELSON, "JIMMIE", "JIMMY" WILLIAMS .

On June 23, 1934, HOMER S. CUMMINGS, Attorney General of the United States, under the authority vested in him by an Act of Congress approved June 6, 1934, offered a reward of

$5,000.00

for the capture of Lester M. Gillis or a reward of

$2,500.00

for information leading to the arrest of Lester M. Gillis.

DESCRIPTION

Age, 25 years; Height, 5 feet 4-3/4 inches; Weight,
133 pounds; Build, medium; Eyes, yellow and grey
slate; Hair, light chestnut; Complexion, light; Occupation, oiler.

All claims to any of the aforesaid rewards and all questions and disputes that may arise as among claimants to the foregoing rewards shall be passed upon by the Attorney General and his decisions shall be final and conclusive. The right is reserved to divide and allocate portions of any of said rewards as between several claimants. No part of the aforesaid rewards shall be paid to any official or employee of the Department of Justice.

If you are in possession of any information concerning the whereabouts of Lester M. Gillis communicate immediately by telephone or telegraph collect to the nearest office of the Division of Investigation, United States Department of Justice, the local offices of which are se forth on the reverse side of this notice.

The apprehension of Lester M. Gillis is sought in connection with the murder of Special Agent W. C. Baum of the Division of Investigation near Rhinelander, Wisconsin on April 23, 1934.

JOHN EDGAR HOOVER, DIRECTOR,
DIVISION OF INVESTIGATION,
UNITED STATES DEPARTMENT OF JUSTICE,
WASHINGTON, D. C.

June 25, 1934

Pint-sized "Baby Face" Nelson, a gunslinger for Dillinger, was sought in 10 states by 5,000 police, 300 infantrymen, the FBI and several airplanes.

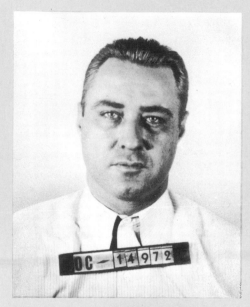

George and Kate Kelly, shown both in mug shots and in a cuddly snapshot, were a husband-and-wife team.

Machine Gun Kelly and His Mrs.

George Kelly, who was so hot with a Tommy gun that he could write his name with bullets on a barn door, started out as a small-time boot-legger. He probably would have stayed small had it not been for the ambition of his wife, Kathryn, an ex-manicurist. Kate pressured her husband into moving up to high-powered capers like bank robbery, kidnaping and murder, and enhanced his prestige among fellow crooks by passing out empty shell casings from his machine gun as souvenirs.

DESCRIPTION

Age, 26 years
Height, 5 feet, 8¼ inches
Weight, 155 pounds
Hair, dark
Eyes, gray
Complexion, medium
Nationality, American
Scars and marks, 1 Vac. cic.
   1 tattoo (Nurse in Rose)

CRIMINAL RECORD

As Charles Arthur Floyd, No. 22318, arrested police department, St. Louis, Missouri, September 16, 1925; charge, highway robbery.
As Charles Floyd, No. 29078, received S.P., Jefferson City, Missouri, December 18, 1925, from St. Louis; crime, robbery, first degree; sentence, 5 years.
As Charles A. Floyd, No. 16950, arrested police department,

Kansas City, Missouri, March 9, 1929; charge, investigation.
As Charles Floyd, No. 9999, arrested police department, Kansas City, Kansas, May 6, 1929; charge, vagrancy and suspicion - highway robbery; released May 7, 1929.
As Charles Floyd, No. 887, arrested police department, Pueblo, Colorado, May 9, 1929; charge, vagrancy; fined $50 and sentenced to serve 60 days in jail.
As Frank Mitchell, No. 19983, arrested police department, Akron, Ohio, March 8, 1930; charge, investigation.
As Charles Arthur Floyd, No. 21458, arrested police department, Toledo, Ohio, May 20, 1930; charge, suspicion.
As Charles Arthur Floyd, sentenced November 24, 1930, to serve from 12 to 15 years in Ohio State Penitentiary (bank robbery, Sylvania, Ohio); escaped enroute to penitentiary.

Charles Arthur Floyd is wanted in connection with the murder of Otto Reed, Chief of Police of McAlester, Oklahoma, William J. Grooms and Frank E. Hermanson, police officers of Kansas City, Missouri, Raymond J. Caffrey, Special Agent of the United States Bureau of Investigation, and their prisoner, Frank Nash, at Kansas City, Missouri, on June 17, 1933.
   Law enforcement agencies kindly transmit any additional information or criminal record to nearest office, United States Bureau of Investigation.
   If apprehended, please notify Special Agent in Charge, United States Bureau of Investigation, 905 Federal Reserve Bank Building, Kansas City, Missouri, and the Director, United States Bureau of Investigation, Department of Justice, Washington, D. C.

(over)   Issued by: J. Edgar Hoover, Director

Gray-eyed and wavy-haired, Floyd was hunted by the FBI for gunning down four lawmen in Kansas City in 1933.

"Pretty Boy" Floyd

An *enfant terrible* of the underworld, Charles Floyd took up crime at age 18 by robbing a local post office of $350 in pennies. During the next 12 years he was reputed to have robbed more than 30 Midwestern banks; in 1932 his score in Oklahoma alone was so high that the state's bank insurance rates doubled. Floyd was equally adept at shooting people. The latter talent gave him such satisfaction that he filed 10 notches in his pocket watch to remind him of the number of men he had killed.

Key members of the Barker gang included "Dock" (top left), Freddie and "Ma", shown with boyfriend Arthur Dunlop.

"Ma" Barker and Her Boys

Arizona Clark "Ma" Barker, who believed in crime for the whole family, reared her four sons to be God-fearing, obedient thugs. Each Sunday she dragged them off to church; weekdays she schooled them in the finer points of thievery, kidnaping and murder. The Barkers shown here, joined by brothers Herman and Lloyd—and occasionally by other gangland luminaries—pulled off so many audacious capers, that they became the all-time leaders in major crime, family style.

The Barrow gang's fondness for hamming in front of a Kodak made identification easier for pursuing lawmen.

Bonnie and Clyde

The most sadistic of the decade's hoods, Clyde Barrow shot down people for the sheer love of killing. He embarked on a murder-and-robbery spree through Missouri, Texas and Oklahoma with his moll, cigar-chomping Bonnie Parker, and a succession of young men. Ill-tempered and somewhat effeminate, Barrow was generally despised by other Midwestern bandits, who felt that his haphazard killings and frequently bungled robberies lowered the standards of the profession.

Clear-eyed, attentive, all his energies focused on the task at hand, Director J. Edgar Hoover of the FBI pursues a hot lead over the telephone.

The Hero Cop

In the decade's running battle between the law and those who broke it, one man emerged as a living folk hero of law enforcement. He was J. Edgar Hoover, the robust, iron-jawed supersleuth who headed the Federal Bureau of Investigation. "Pick a small boy these days and ask him who of all the people in the world he wants to be like," wrote the New York *World-Telegram* in 1936, "and ten to one he will reply—J. Edgar Hoover."

Hoover was the perfect hero. Nearly six feet tall, sturdily built, with penetrating, coal-black eyes and thick, wiry hair, he seemed the very image of clean-living, hard-driving Americanism. His walk was brisk and military. When he spoke, his words came out in crisp, staccato bursts, like the rattle of a Tommy gun. As he led his crack army of some 600 hand-picked G-men against the underworld, taking on such daredevil outlaws as John Dillinger and "Pretty Boy" Floyd, the nation's top cop seemed far more dashing than the top robbers he was out to catch.

Hoover fought crime with a vitality that was almost compulsive. "The Director," as he liked being called, would tackle a dozen fast-breaking cases at once, shooting a barrage of teletype messages to his 37 field offices about the country, barking orders over his battery of telephones, while at the same time writing his own speeches and reports and handling much of the Bureau's correspondence himself. Sometimes, as when he nabbed Alvin (Old Creepy) Karpis, one-time paramour of the matronly killer "Ma" Barker, the Director would strap on his .45 and charge in at the head of his troops to personally arrest a particularly notorious crook.

The Director's close associates professed themselves to be awed by his energy. "When a big case is on he has often sat at his desk for 72 hours at a stretch," marveled a friend, writer Herbert Corey; and Hoover's boss, Attorney General Homer Cummings, warned him: "You will burn yourself out." But Director Hoover refused to let up. "The job is never done," he would exclaim, in one of the manly clichés that spiced his conversations.

No Boy Scout had fewer vices than the FBI chief. He hardly ever smoked, drank only moderately and was never known to tell an off-color story. His principal diversions were awesomely wholesome and American: baseball and fishing. He had a weakness for boardinghouse gourmandizing, a hearty platter of corned beef and cabbage being his favorite. But he tried to make up for it with a regimen of weight-lifting and light-footed gymnastics at the FBI gym. His only visible eccentricity—a fondness for collecting delicate blown glass and other early American antiques—was itself a model of dedicated patriotism.

On those rare evenings when he was not working late at the Bureau, Hoover would stay at home in his study, reading law enforcement comic strips, such as *Dick Tracy* and *Secret Agent X-9*, or browsing through Jack London's adventure stories. A bachelor, he lived with his elderly mother and pet dog in the same modest frame house in Washington, D.C., where in 1895 he had been born. His few close friends were mostly FBI staffers such as office assistant Clyde Tolson and gun expert Frank Baughman. He had never been known to take a girl on a date. Such fri-

---

We cannot forget that an army of 200,000 persons who will commit murder before they die roams America.

J. EDGAR HOOVER TO THE HOLY NAME SOCIETY, 1936

---

volity might give the FBI a bad name; and in any case the Director had little time for romance. For he was wedded to his work, and the FBI was a jealous wife.

Hoover's love affair with the FBI had been a hot item years before the decade began. A George Washington Law School graduate, he became Special Assistant to Attorney General Mitchell A. Palmer in 1919, and two years later he was appointed Assistant Director of the embryo FBI. At that time the Bureau was a relatively obscure branch of the Justice Department. It had been set up in 1908 as the Attorney General's private gumshoe operation, at one point reportedly being used by Teddy Roosevelt to snoop on opposition Senators. By the 1920s, it was still handling only such mundane tasks as uncovering federal bank frauds and pursuing violators of the anti-prostitution Mann Act. When the Directorship fell vacant in 1924, the vigorous 29-year-old Hoover succeeded to the top spot.

The new Director began immediately to throw his weight around. The organization he headed had degenerated into a shambles during the Harding era. In fact, the entire Department of Justice had become known as the Department of Easy Virtue. Harding's Attorney General, Harry M. Daugherty, had used the Bureau to give

I shall continue to direct the attention of the American public toward the filthy mess which sentimentalists, influenced political appointees, persons of inefficiency and others afflicted with an itching palm have made of parole. HOOVER IN *PERSONS IN HIDING,* 1936

jobs to party hacks, no matter how bizarre their qualifications. One man had been handed an agent's badge for supplying chorus girls to a top administration official, another for singing ribald songs outside the Justice Department building during lunch hour. Many agents had close underworld contacts; some were ex-convicts, others engaged in wholesale graft and bootlegging. One particularly unsavory federal sleuth was Gaston B. Means, an expert at conning rich widows. He had been indicted once, for forging the will of an elderly matron who owned a fortune in timber. Later, during the Lindbergh kidnaping, he scandalized the nation by bilking $100,000 out of a dowager who had hired him to find the missing baby.

Hoover's first major official act was to fire a third of the Bureau, beginning with Means. ("The man had always disgusted me," he said.) "The Bureau must be divorced from politics and not a catch-all for political hacks," Hoover intoned. "Appointments must be made on merit."

He then decreed stiff qualifications for Bureau employees. All agents would need a degree in law or accounting and would have to pass a competitive entrance exam. A character check then scratched all but the "decent, honorable, respectable young men." "We can't afford merely to be right," Hoover said. "We must give every *appearance* of doing right to avoid criticism."

The appearance the new agents did give was unimpeachably clean cut. "One somehow gets an impression

that they are just hoping that some ruffian will make a slurring remark about motherhood or some such sacred subject, so that they can toss him into the gutter with a jujitsu flick of the wrist," observed the *New Yorker* in 1937.

Before becoming full-fledged agents, applicants were subjected to a tough, three-month training course in crime-fighting techniques devised by Hoover. They were also handed a code of conduct which, among other strait-laced admonitions, warned against taking a drink on duty. A bit of FBI folklore held that if ever an agent's thirst got too great, he would go to his hotel room, pull the curtains, lock the door and hang his coat over the keyhole. He would then flick out the lights, creep under the bed and take his nip. Having imbibed, he would turn the lights back on, go to the bureau, stare deep into the mirror and say, "You're a liar. I did not."

With the rules laid down, the young Director began to run his Washington office like a military command post. "When he is aroused his voice cracks like a teamster's whip," observed one reporter. His field agents were on call 24 hours a day, and Hoover sent out special inspectors who dropped in unannounced to check on his men. When working on a hot case every G-man was required to phone Washington hourly, so that Hoover could spot their positions with pins on a wall map opposite his desk.

By 1930 the hard-driving Director had turned his Bureau into the most effective crime-fighting machine since the invention of the six-gun. He had gathered a file of some three million fingerprints at a time when most local police forces still identified miscreants by complicated and highly fallible measurements of their skull and arm bones. Another Hoover innovation was a crime laboratory for examining car tracks, expended bullets, blood stains, hair, fabric, and other shreds of evidence.

Despite all this super-organization, in early 1932, hardly anyone outside the government had yet heard of the FBI. Its jurisdiction was still limited by law to substantially the same dreary federal chores, so that Hoover's sleek bloodhounds, like their sleazy predecessors, spent most of their time on the trail of prostitutes, chiselers and violators of such arcane statutes as the Migratory Birds Act. Even in this limited area the G-men could not make arrests, but had to call the local cops for the pinch. Nor were the Feds permitted to carry guns.

Then, quite suddenly, the nation was jolted by a series of spectacular crimes, beginning with the Lindbergh kidnaping *(page 100)*. A whole new race of hoodlums *(pages 101-107)* seemed to rise up, and alarming statistics began to appear in the news: America had the highest homicide rate in the civilized world; the nation's banks were being robbed at the rate of two a day; crime was costing each American $140 a year. And the Justice Department claimed that there were 400,000 hoods loose in America.

Furthermore, state and local police were simply not able to cope with the epidemic of kidnapings, bank robberies, homicides and extortion rackets. Often, while tracking down a gang, the cops would find that the quarry had slipped into the next state and hence out of their jurisdiction. Clearly, something radical needed to be done. The worst alarmists suggested that martial law be declared and the Army called in. J. Edgar Hoover had a better idea: his FBI was ready and able to tackle the job. All he needed was an okay from Congress, removing the limitations on FBI tactics and enlarging the number of federal crimes on which the Bureau could act.

Moving quickly, Congress in mid-1932 passed the "Lindbergh Law" which for all practical purposes made

---

Here is a battle between priceless God-fearing principles on the one hand and pagan ideals and godlessness on the other. . . .

In these troubled days, when you strengthen the hand of law enforcement, you add power to the muscles of liberty.

HOOVER TO *TIME* MAGAZINE, 1939

---

snatching a federal crime, thus allowing the G-men to chase kidnapers. Other new laws followed. Robberies of national banks, thefts of more than $5,000 carried out across state lines, illegal use of telephone and telegraph wires, assaults on federal officers and crossing state lines to avoid testifying in court were all made federal offen-

ses. Virtually any other type of crime that crossed a state line became fair game for the G-men. Furthermore, the bans against making arrests and carrying firearms were lifted, and the G-men began to trade shot for shot with the best of the gunslinging hoodlums.

Moving at a full gallop, Hoover's posse of crimebusters began running down desperadoes. They quickly nailed:

- John Dillinger, Public Enemy No. 1. A Chicago brothelkeeper betrayed Dillinger to the Feds and in July of 1934, in front of a Chicago movie house, an attack force led by G-man Melvin Purvis gunned him down.
- "Baby Face" Nelson, a particularly vicious pal of Dillinger's. Nelson was spotted while driving through a Chicago suburb in November 1934. During the ensuing gun battle he was fatally wounded, but he also took the lives of the two federal agents who were arresting him.
- Charles "Pretty Boy" Floyd—shot to death while battling G-men on an Ohio farm in October 1934.
- Arizona Clark "Ma" Barker, who died with her son Freddie while trying to outshoot federal agents besieging her hideout in Oklawaha, Florida, in 1935.
- George "Machine Gun" Kelly, who was responsible for giving the federal investigators their nickname. In 1933 Hoover's agents, seeking Kelly for the kidnaping of Oklahoma City oilman Charles F. Urschel, crashed into his hideout to arrest him. He yelled, "Don't shoot, G-men, don't shoot!" Asked why he had called them "G-men," he said it was short for Government men.

Others, less notorious but no less colorful, fell to the G-men. There was, for one, "Bla Bla the Black Man," who ran a car-theft ring in Brooklyn and shipped so many stolen autos to Europe that at one point he flooded the market, and prices fell. Brooklyn police could pin nothing on him. But the FBI was called in and unearthed the cable address the master car-thief used in his European export business. Bla Bla was hauled in and convicted, and insurance on cars in Brooklyn dropped 15 per cent.

As the record mounted, Hoover and his agents became the heroes of the day. "The nation has waited with the patience of a Job for this hour," extolled the St. Louis *Post*

Dispatch. "In a determined Department of Justice backed by the resources of the national Government, gangsters face an invincible foe." Hollywood got into the act, and in 1935 Warner Brothers premiered *G-Men*, in which James Cagney as the intrepid agent brought to justice the nation's worst public enemy and got the girl as well. (The latter feat was not generally considered part of the job for real live G-men, as the Director's own opinion of women as companions had not thawed.) Meanwhile, small boys all over the country began wearing tin G-man badges, toting toy Tommy guns, wearing G-man underwear and sleeping in G-man pajamas. Hoover himself was showered with honorary degrees from colleges ranging in renown from New York University to Kalamazoo College in Michigan. Other honors bestowed upon him included a Distinguished Service Medal offered by the Boys Clubs of America and the Order of the Star of Romania.

Warming to the glare of the limelight, the tight-lipped Hoover climbed the lecture platform to make pronouncements on virtually anything that occurred to him. For example, he told one audience that mothers who played bridge instead of minding the kids were responsible for a rising tide of juvenile delinquency. The Director hurled rhetorical vitriol at the nation's criminals, calling them "mad dogs with guns in their hands and murder in their hearts," and "scum from the boiling pot of the underworld." "Don't call or refer to the country's outstanding criminals as 'public enemies,'" he warned the graduating class at the University of Maryland in 1936. "I suggest that they be called 'public rats.'"

In the course of his scoldings, the Director summoned up fresh batches of wildly fluctuating scare statistics. In March 1936 he referred to the "armed forces of crime which number more than 3 million." Three months later he set the figure at 500,000, "a whole half-million of armed thugs, murderers, thieves, firebugs, assassins, robbers and hold-up men." Some six months after that, the army of crime had zoomed back up to 3.5 million.

The Director also tried his hand at writing. In 1938 he published *Persons in Hiding*, an account of some of the Bu-

reau's more notable successes. Though the public bought thousands of copies, reviewers gave it a drubbing for its preachy tone and stylistic pomposities. "If he is writing he never calls fishing 'fishing,'" Cal Tinney declared in the New York *Post*. "To him it's 'piscatorial diversion.'"

Undaunted, Hoover intensified his fire in a new broadside of speeches aimed not only at crooks, but at anyone who, he felt, sympathized with them. This included "shyster lawyers and other legal vermin," "sob-sister judges," political liberals and other "sentimental moo-cows" who believed in lightening the sentences of "criminal jackals." He also had some choice words for professional politicians: "The bullets of the underworld are today poisoned by the verdigris of politics."

It was remarks like these that first threatened to trip up the sure-footed Director, who suddenly began to hear indignant voices from sources other than the underworld. Powerful government officials began to feel that Hoover was getting just a bit too big for his breeches. Tennessee's Senator Kenneth McKeller, in a move in 1936 to cut FBI funds, told Hoover: "It seems to me your department is just running wild." Jim Farley, President Roosevelt's Postmaster General and one-time campaign manager, was reported in 1934 by a Washington gossip columnist to have tried to get Hoover fired. Besides eliminating an ir-

---

Crime is a dangerous, cancerous condition which, if not curbed and beaten down, will soon eat at the very vitals of the country.

HOOVER TO THE UNIVERSITY OF MARYLAND, 1936

---

ritant, Farley was said to have wanted to use FBI jobs to pay off political debts. Hoover fought back by having the Postmaster General's phone tapped.

Local police officers, who had welcomed the Feds' response to their SOS a few years before, now started to complain that Hoover was grabbing too much limelight. One local news story claimed the Director was nothing but a publicity hound, a "David Belasco in a squad car."

In New York particularly, during the latter half of the decade, the FBI chief was becoming *persona summa non grata.* In December 1936 the city police and the FBI had traced bank robber and kidnaper Harry Brunette to a West Side apartment. The FBI, with Hoover in personal command, charged ahead to make the capture. In the ensuing shoot-'em-up, the G-men set fire to the building with a tear-gas grenade. And when the smoke had all blown away, firemen called to the scene claimed that the G-men had carelessly lobbed a few shots in their direction.

The bad feeling in New York came to a head in 1939, when Hoover managed to get credit for nabbing Louis "Lepke" Buchalter, Manhattan racket czar and boss of Murder, Inc. An ambitious district attorney, Tom Dewey, had been trying to nail Buchalter himself for murder, vice-peddling, and for running a multi-million-dollar extortion racket. In 1939 Dewey announced a $25,000 reward for his capture. Buchalter then became uneasy that one of his pals might turn him in to face Dewey's murder rap. The hoodlum therefore decided to surrender to the FBI, which wanted him only for drug smuggling.

To set up the pinch Buchalter called columnist Walter Winchell, a friend of Hoover's. On the night of August 24, 1939, Winchell picked up Buchalter at Madison Square, and drove him to a spot on Fifth Avenue where a black limousine was idling. The columnist escorted the racketeer to the car and introduced him to the man inside. "Mr. Hoover, this is Lepke," he said. "How do you do," said Hoover, and Buchalter responded, "Glad to meet you."

Naturally the story was splashed all over Winchell's column. And naturally, Dewey was furious at being upstaged.

Quite apart from such personal vendettas, many Americans grew concerned that the zealous Hoover might be encroaching on civil liberties. Senator George Norris of Nebraska expressed the fear in 1940 that the FBI was turning into an "American OGPU," a home-grown version of Soviet Russia's dreaded secret police. Other well-informed people remembered the 1909 rumors of Teddy Roosevelt's Senate snooping. Was it true, now, that the FBI kept secret dossiers on government officials and prominent liberals? Other skeletons were dragged from their tombs: in 1919, under Attorney General Mitchell

Palmer, the Bureau had rounded up thousands of harmless citizens, without warrants, on the suspicion that they might be Communists or anarchists. People also recalled that the man who prosecuted the suspects had been Palmer's eager young assistant—J. Edgar Hoover. Now, toward the end of the '30s, the Justice Department was again in full cry against various radicals. Would there be a repeat of the Palmer raids?

Never, Hoover declared: "The FBI will always strive to preserve the civil liberties of every American citizen.

Intellectual license and debauchery is un-American. In righteous indignation it is time to drive the debauchers of America out in the open.

HOOVER TO THE NATIONAL CONVENTION OF THE AMERICAN LEGION, 1940

We can never become [an OGPU] or a Gestapo." His detractors had "mental halitosis," he claimed, and the campaign to malign him was a Red plot: "Communists at a meeting yesterday in New York have instructed two of their best writers to portray me as a Broadway glamorboy and particularly to inquire into my affairs with women in New York," he told TIME magazine in 1940.

Aside from such noisily satisfying counterfire, Hoover could take solace from the fact that, in an era when there was still a fairly clear line between the good guys and the bad guys, most ordinary Americans admired him and shared his beliefs about the need for law and order. His hard-handed campaign against the Communists and, of course, fascists—which he called "two twin horrid, spectral growths of alien soil and an alien spirit," seemed justifiable during the uncertain days when a second world war was gathering momentum in Europe. But at the close of the decade the Director maintained that he derived his greatest comfort from a framed text which he kept on top of the radio in his office, and which read in part:

"In every field of human endeavor, he that is first must perpetually live in the white light of publicity. . . . When a man's work becomes a standard for the whole world, it also becomes a target for the shafts of the envious few."

F.D.R.

ABOLISH BREAD LINES
VOTE FOR
ROOSEVELT

F.D.R. campaigns in Indianapolis, October 1932.

That Man in the White House

Never was there such a change in the transfer of a government. The President is the boss, the dynamo, the works. ARTHUR KROCK IN *THE NEW YORK TIMES*, MARCH 12, 1933

When Franklin D. Roosevelt became the 32nd President of the United States, the country was scared, more scared than ever in its history. That very morning, March 4, 1933, every last bank in the nation had had to close its doors. The old leaders were ashen-faced. "I'm afraid," said the chairman of Bethlehem Steel, Charles Schwab, "every man is afraid."

On the high inaugural platform in front of the Capitol, the 51-year-old President-elect repeated the oath of office in a clear, deliberate voice, looked out over the tense throng covering 10 acres of lawn and pavement and said: "This Nation asks for action, and action now." Entering his car to go to the White House, he clasped his strong hands over his head in the salute of a champion. The next morning, rolling in a wheelchair as he had since he was crippled by polio 12 years before, Roosevelt moved into the oval office of Presidents. He sat alone for a few moments, then gave a great shout for his aides and began to act, starting with a call for a special session of Congress. His emergency banking bill strengthening the nation's financial system roared through the House unchanged in 38 minutes. When the banks reopened four days later, deposits exceeded withdrawals. The immediate panic was over. The nation's confidence was beginning to return.

Sensing opportunity, F.D.R. kept the lawmakers in session. In the next 100 days, riding herd on the uneasy nation with a firmer rein than it had felt since the days of his cousin, Teddy Roosevelt, he permanently altered the conduct of American life. Fifteen major messages streamed from the White House to Capitol Hill. When Congress adjourned on June 16, fifteen new laws assured concerted government action: to employ the jobless, to develop the backward Tennessee Valley, to support crop prices, to repeal Prohibition, to stop home foreclosures, to insure bank deposits, to stabilize the economy, and more.

F.D.R. called the program a "New Deal" for the nation, but others thought it went beyond that. "We have had our revolution," said *Collier's* magazine. "We like it." The people raised their heads; even the well-to-do were at first delighted. As Roosevelt had noted, action, any kind of action, had been their plea. Kansas' Republican governor, Alf Landon, had said: "Even the iron hand of a dictator is in preference to a paralytic stroke." Now industrialist Pierre du Pont sent F.D.R. a friendly letter. And press lord William Randolph Hearst flattered F.D.R.: "I guess at your next election we will make it unanimous."

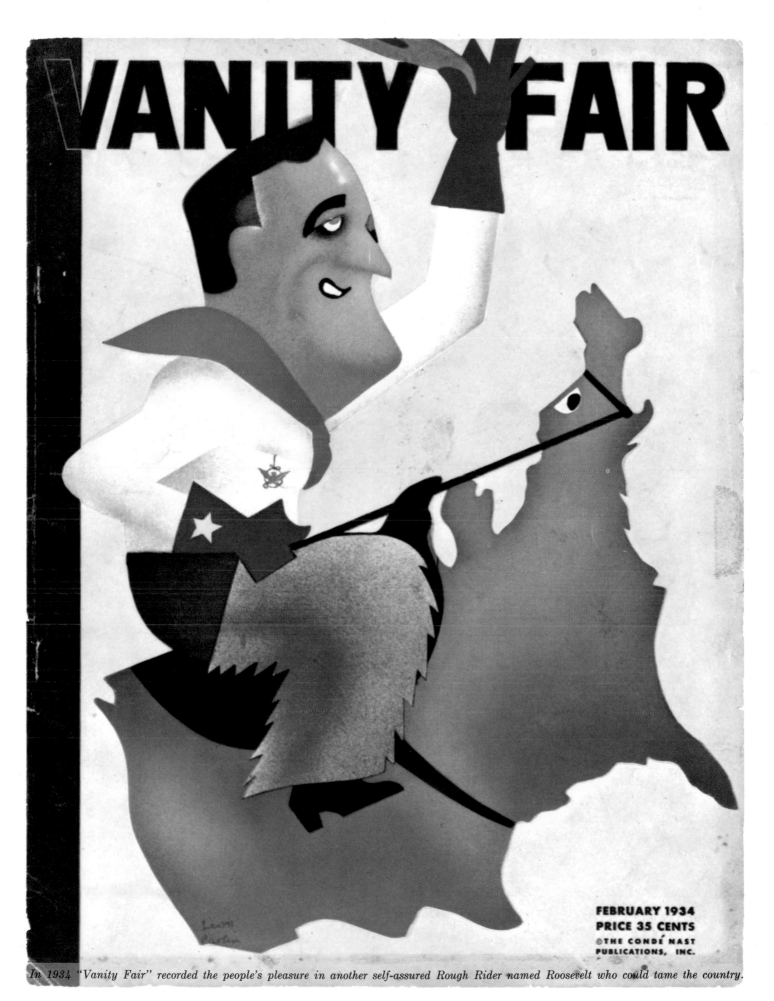

VANITY FAIR

FEBRUARY 1934
PRICE 35 CENTS
©THE CONDÉ NAST
PUBLICATIONS, INC.

In 1934 "Vanity Fair" recorded the people's pleasure in another self-assured Rough Rider named Roosevelt who could tame the country.

F.D.R. and his wife, Eleanor, were both energetic, strong-willed and independent. She believed he might have been happier with a less critical wife.

The Look of the New Family

The second family of Roosevelts to move into the White House within a quarter century was an exciting batch of individualists with lots of verve and offspring *(below)*. Each of F.D.R.'s children tended to go his own way, but Christmas Eve always found the clan gathered. Surrounded by grandchildren, F.D.R. read from Dickens' *A Christmas Carol,* acting out the parts of Scrooge and Tiny Tim with gusto. Next day, at Christmas dinner, he carved paper-thin slices of turkey, boasting "You can almost *read* through it." As the Presidency wore on, however, Roosevelt had less and less time for family matters. One day when a distraught son poured out his troubles, F.D.R. absently handed him a paper, saying: "This is a most important document—I should like to have your opinion on it."

A Spreading Tree

ANNA • JAMES • ELLIOTT • FRANKLIN JR. • JOHN

CURTIS DALL • JOHN BOETTIGER • BETSY CUSHING • ELIZABETH DONNER • RUTH GOOGINS • ETHEL DU PONT • ANNE CLARK

SISTIE • JOHN • SARA • WILLIAM • RUTH • FRANKLIN III

BUZZIE • KATE • ELLIOTT JR.

F.D.R.'s children tended to marry young and to reproduce often. By decade's end the record was: seven marriages, two divorces, nine youngsters.

In old sweater and flannels, F.D.R. takes James sailing on the "Amberjack II." Sailing, he told Harold Ickes, was the only way he could really rest.

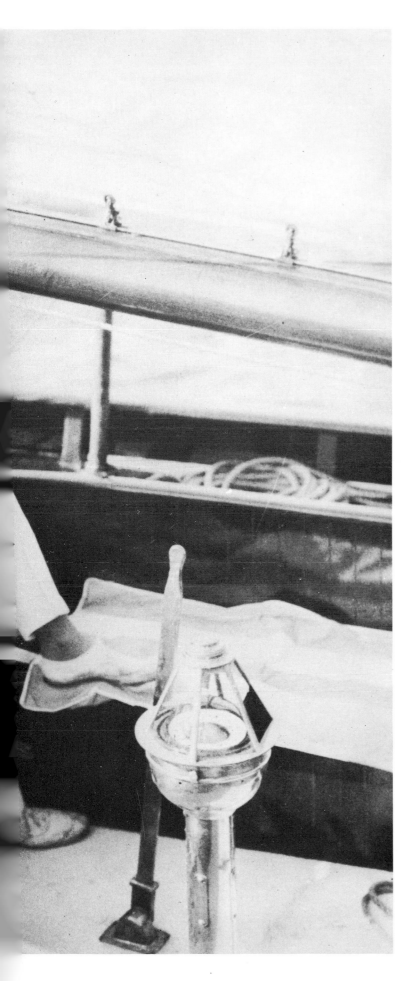

F.D.R. loved the sea. Not only did it restore him after the burdens of office but it gave him a chance to restore his relationships with his children. Joyously he wrote back from a cruise: "The boys are having a grand time and we have one continuous kidding match." In 1934 he took Franklin Jr. and John on a 14,000-mile voyage aboard the cruiser *Houston.* They ranged from Haiti to Hawaii and F.D.R. got another chance, denied him in Washington, to spend lazy hours with his boys. He reported home to his wife, who had long since given up sailing for horseback riding, "The boys are grand and really love it I think."

After a morning ride Mrs. F.D.R. plays with Sistie and Buzzie Dall.

F.D.R. howls along with (from left) son James, William McAdoo and advisor James Farley as Will Rogers gets off a sly introduction in 1932.

The Style of the New President

The new President surprised a lot of people. Before the election the best thinkers considered him a lightweight —"a pleasant man who, without any important qualifications, would very much like to be President," as pundit Walter Lippmann wrote. But the critics soon realized that F.D.R.'s easy quips and laughter reflected not vacuous amiability but buoyant confidence, that here was a tough-minded man with a quick grasp of what had to be done. Accordingly Lippmann, for one, ate crow: "The nation which had lost confidence in everything and everybody has regained confidence in the government and in itself."

"How do you account for him?" gasped Kansas editor William Allen White. "Was I just fooled before the election, or has he developed?" The quotations below from cowboy entertainer-philosopher Will Rogers expressed the nation's delight at the new man in the White House.

---

*A*merica hasn't been as happy in three years as they are today, no money, no banks, no work, no nothing, but they know they got a man in there who is wise to Congress, wise to our so-called big men. The whole country is with him, just so he does something. If he burned down the capitol, we would cheer and say "well, we at least got a fire started anyhow."

MARCH 5, 1933

Mr. Roosevelt is a terribly plain spoken man. Remember the speech that night about the banks. Long adjectives and nouns he dident mess with 'em at all. He knows what the country wants is relief and not rhetoric. He is the first Harvard man to know enough to drop three syllables when he has something to say. Why compared to me he is almost illiterate.

MAY 7, 1933

I will say one thing for this Administration. It's the only time when the fellow with money is worrying more than the one without it.

OCTOBER 3, 1933

The Team

LEFT WING

| REX TUGWELL | FRANCES PERKINS | HENRY WALLACE | HARRY HOPKINS | HENRY MORGENTHAU |
| Agriculture | Labor | Agriculture | Federal Relief | Treasury |

Let's concentrate upon one thing. Save the people and the nation and, if we have to change our minds twice every day to accomplish that end, we should do it.

F.D.R. TO COMMERCE SECRETARY DAN ROPER

If he became convinced tomorrow that coming out for cannibalism would get him the votes he so sorely needs, he would begin fattening a missionary in the White House backyard come Wednesday. H.L. MENCKEN

It is almost impossible to come to grips with him. HAROLD ICKES

The New Deal turned Washington from a placid Southern town into an exciting, pulsating seat of power and attracted all sorts of bright, opinionated men with all sorts of new ideas. They came to help F.D.R. remake America, and he reveled in their minds—listening, taking fast decisions, cutting corners. Pragmatism was the game and F.D.R. called the plays: "Take a method and try it. If it fails, try another. But above all, try something."

The team pictured in the *Vanity Fair* montage above represented F.D.R.'s lineup of key players at the end of his first year. Some were quickly benched. The favorite at this time, conservative Lewis Douglas, protested one day that failure to balance the budget meant the end of Western civilization—and was heard of no more. Some

RIGHT WING

CAPTAIN					
FRANKLIN D. ROOSEVELT	HUGH JOHNSON	DANIEL ROPER	GEORGE PEEK	LEWIS DOUGLAS	HAROLD ICKES
President	NRA	Commerce	Farming Controls	Budget	Interior

hardy souls lasted: Harold Ickes of Interior, grumpy, incorruptible; Henry Wallace of Agriculture, his farm boots in manure and his head in the clouds; hard-boiled but socially sensitive relief chief Harry Hopkins; Madame Frances Perkins of Labor, the first woman in a U.S. Cabinet.

It was a cocky team, but F.D.R. was captain and if the gang would not arrive at a conclusion, he would say: "Put them in a room and tell them no lunch."

Yet while his men and methods shifted, not so F.D.R.'s motives. As he picked his way, now turning right, now left, not hesitating to be devious when it suited him, he kept moving toward the goals in his mind—and his mind was strong and stubborn. He rammed through such controversial reforms as Social Security. As the country

began to regain confidence, however, F.D.R. found the going tougher. He suffered more defeats. But even in defeat, F.D.R. managed to keep gaining ground. Thus, though he failed in 1937 to pack the Supreme Court with liberal Justices, within months a majority of the nine-man Court, seeing the handwriting on the wall, upheld both the New Dealing Wagner Labor Act and minimum wage laws. F.D.R. kept on losing occasional yardage to an increasingly contentious Congress. Nevertheless, by the end of the decade the overall game had been won. More people had jobs, the economy was alive and breathing and, though many of the old team had departed Washington, Roosevelt was still a strong captain who had persuaded a revived country to play by his rules.

The Personal Touch

In the '30s George M. Cohan, star of the Broadway musical "I'd Rather Be Right," used to break up the audience by saying: "Bring me another fireside, I'm going on the air." Everyone knew he was joshing F.D.R.'s own personal bit of show biz—the Fireside Chats. These were informal radio talks F.D.R. delivered to the nation as Americans were relaxing after dinner. It was his favorite way of selling his programs and, in the face of Establishment and press hostility, it was indispensable in winning support for the New Deal. When F.D.R.'s calm, resonant voice intoned "My Friends," most Americans felt they were.

Inevitably, the Fireside Chats invited spoofing, some of it nasty, some as gentle as Cohan's wisecrack and the 1935 *Esquire* cartoon at right, showing F.D.R.'s wife Eleanor looking on as he broadcasts while his grandchildren badger him to hurry and get off the air. But the Fireside Chats were deadly serious, both for F.D.R. and for the country. The first one, explaining the bank crisis, was decisive in reversing the panic. Here, in part, is what people heard on their radios that evening of March 12, 1933.

I want to tell you what has been done in the last few days, why it was done, and what the next steps are going to be. First of all, let me state the simple fact that when you deposit money in a bank the bank does not put the money into a safe deposit vault. It invests your money in many different forms of credit—bonds, mortgages. In other words, the bank puts your money to work to keep the wheels turning around. A comparatively small part of the money is kept in currency—sufficient to cover the cash needs of the average citizen. In other words, the total amount of all the currency in the country is only a small fraction of the total deposits in all of the banks. What, then, happened? Because of undermined confidence, there was a general rush to turn bank deposits into currency. On the spur of the moment it was, of course, impossible to sell perfectly sound assets of a bank and convert them into cash except at panic prices far below their real value.

It was then that I issued the proclamation for the nationwide bank holiday. The second step was the legislation passed by the Congress to extend the holiday and lift the ban of that holiday gradually. This law also gave authority to develop a program of rehabilitation of our banking facilities. The new law allows the twelve Federal Reserve Banks to issue additional currency backed by actual, good assets. As a result, we start tomorrow, Monday, opening banks in the twelve Federal Reserve Bank cities—banks which have already been found to be all right. On succeeding days banks in smaller places will resume business, subject, of course, to the Government's physical ability to make common sense checkups. When the banks resume a very few people who have not recovered from their fear may again begin withdrawals. Let me make clear that the banks will take care of all needs —and it is my belief that when the people find that they can get their money the phantom of fear will soon be laid. I assure you that it is safer to keep your money in a reopened bank than under the mattress.

There will be, of course, some banks unable to open without being reorganized. The new law allows the Government to assist in making these reorganizations quickly and effectively. I do not promise you that every bank will be reopened or that individual losses will not be suffered, but there will be no losses that possibly could have been avoided; and there would have been greater losses had we continued to drift. I can even promise you salvation for some at least of the sorely pressed banks. Confidence and courage are the essentials in our plan. You must have faith; you must not be stampeded by rumors. We have provided the machinery to restore our financial system; it is up to you to support and make it work. Together we cannot fail.

AW, GEE, GRAN'POP, YOU'RE RUNNIN' OVER INTO ED WYNN'S PROGRAM!

The Alphabet Agencies: NRA

As F.D.R. put his New Deal into effect, Congress spawned dozens of acts and agencies to carry the government's new burdens. Given long names, these organizations became known by their initials, which, added together, made up an entire alphabet of recovery measures. The office that excited the fiercest partisanship was the NRA (National Recovery Administration), created to regulate wages, working hours and, indirectly, prices.

Most ordinary Americans greeted NRA enthusiastically. Posters with the Blue Eagle symbol were splashed everywhere, and big cities staged monster rallies to show support of the NRA codes. In New York, 250,000 people marched up Fifth Avenue to the music of 200 bands. In Tulsa, the hometown of NRA director Hugh Johnson, his 77-year-old mother led a parade and warned: "People had better obey the NRA because my son will enforce it like lightning, and you can never tell when lightning will strike." As columnist Heywood Broun prophesied, these parades had a lasting issue of new hope and confidence: "When a line forms and your shoulder touches that of a fellow and a comrade, solidarity is about to be born."

Nevertheless, New Deal opponents kept up a barrage of criticism. Businessmen damned NRA as "creeping socialism," while union men called it "business fascism." The Hearst newspapers suggested bitterly that what the initials NRA really stood for was: "No Recovery Allowed."

The NRA emblem appeared on any usable empty space.

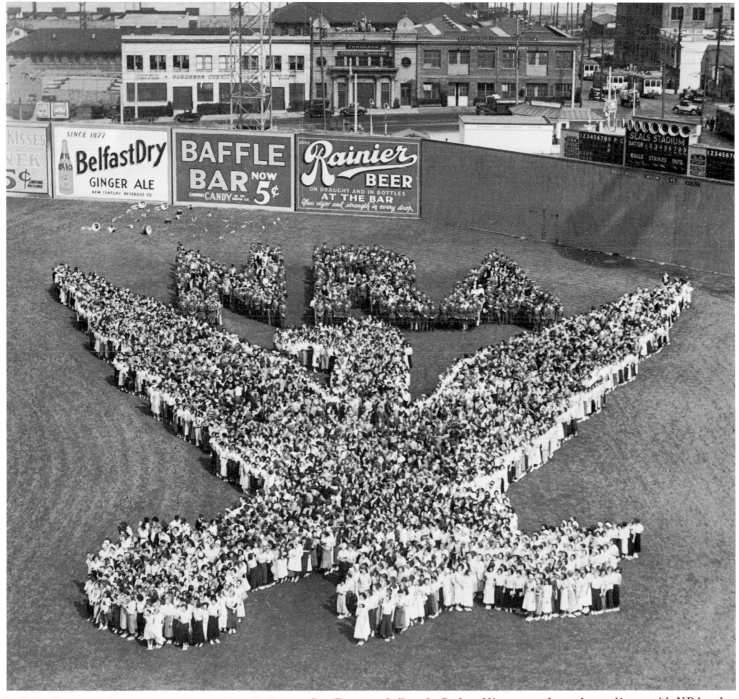

Rallying for NRA, 8,000 children form a giant eagle in a San Francisco ball park. Such public support fostered compliance with NRA codes.

CCC boys give three cheers at Camp Dix, New Jersey, after their first day. The average enlistee was a 20-year-old from a large family on relief.

CCC

Not even the angriest opponents of the New Deal had much to say against the good works initiated by the CCC (Civilian Conservation Corps). In its nine years of existence, the CCC took some 2.5 million young men from the ranks of the unemployed, paid them $30 a month (most of it automatically sent to the home folks) and put them to work planting 200 million trees, fighting pine-twig blight and Dutch elm disease, digging drainage ditches and fish ponds, building firebreaks and reservoirs, clearing beaches and camping grounds, and even restoring historic battlefields. This massive effort of conservation and reforestation benefited not only the nation but the boys themselves. One declared, "It made a man of me all right." Said another man: "If a boy wants to go and get a job after he's been in the C's, he'll know how to work."

The U.S. Army and the Forest Service jointly supervised the CCC.

PWA

To make jobs and stimulate business, F.D.R. in 1933 convinced Congress to create the federally financed PWA (Public Works Administration)—and thereby changed the face of America. Armies of workmen for PWA built a water supply system for Denver; a flood control system for Ohio's Muskingum Valley; a port for Brownsville, Texas; roads and bridges connecting Key West with the Florida mainland. A sampling of other PWA projects appears on these pages—but only a small sampling. Between 1933 and 1939 PWA invested more than six billion dollars and 4.75 billion man-hours of labor in constructing about 10 per cent of all the new transportation facilities built in the United States during the period, 35 per cent of the new hospitals and health facilities, 65 per cent of the city halls and courthouses and sewage disposal plants, and 70 per cent of all educational buildings.

Because these projects were slow in developing, F.D.R. complemented PWA with a nominally confusing addition to his alphabet soup, the WPA (Works Progress Administration). The main difference between the two agencies was that PWA simply financed the projects, whereas WPA handled the entire operation. In addition, WPA found a new way to use its huge appropriations by making the federal government a big-time patron of the arts (overleaf).

MUNICIPAL FERRYBOAT, NEW YORK CITY

ELECTRIFICATION OF PENNSYLVANIA RAILROAD

PAVILION, HUNTINGTON BEACH, CALIFORNIA

WORK SHED, GRAND CANYON NATIONAL PARK

MENTAL HOSPITAL, CAMARILLO, CALIFORNIA

SAN FRANCISCO FAIR CONSTRUCTION

LINCOLN TUNNEL, NEW YORK—NEW JERSEY

GOLD DEPOSITORY, FORT KNOX, KENTUCKY

TRIBOROUGH BRIDGE, NEW YORK CITY

MALL, WASHINGTON, D.C.

PRISON FARM, TATTNALL COUNTY, GEORGIA

BOULDER DAM, COLORADO RIVER

ZOO, WASHINGTON, D.C.

SWIMMING POOL, WHEELING, WEST VIRGINIA

BAND SHELL, PHOENIX, ARIZONA

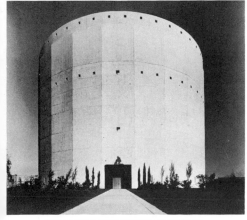

WATER TANK, SACRAMENTO, CALIFORNIA

FLORAL CONSERVATORY, ST. LOUIS

FEDERAL TRADE COMMISSION, WASHINGTON, D.C.

WPA

Following the thesis that whenever possible a jobless man should be put in his own line of work, the WPA recruited thousands of unemployed artists and assigned them to projects paying up to $94.90 a month. Composers composed; musical anthropologists toured backwoods America recording folk songs; actors for the Federal Theatre entertained some 30 million people with shows. By decade's end, a whole generation of painters and writers had served its apprenticeship on the WPA. Admittedly, some artists were assigned work of questionable value. One writer made his bread and butter by taking a census of dogs in California's Monterey Peninsula. In 1939 the name of that writer and of his first major novel became household words: John Steinbeck and *The Grapes of Wrath*.

Actors sing in "The Swing Mikado," one of 1,200 WPA productions.

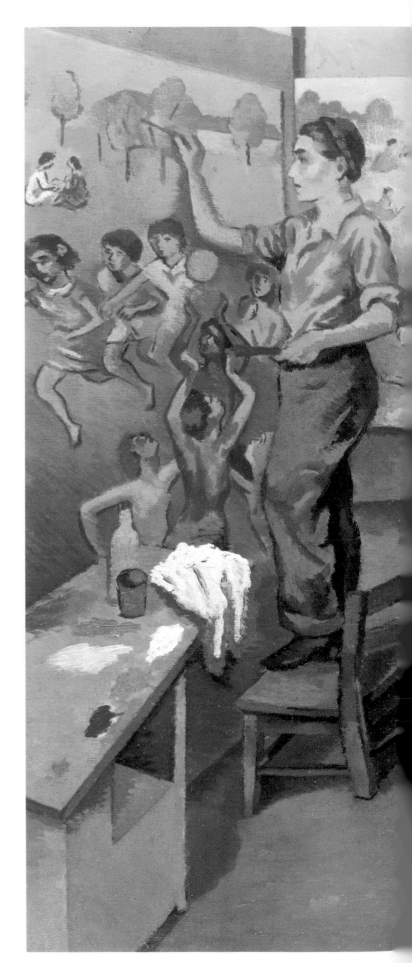

WPA artists are depicted at work by colleague Moses Soyer. Other WPA painters were Jackson Pollock, Willem de Kooning and Ben Shahn.

Cheers and Catcalls

Nobody in the '30s ever said he just guessed F.D.R. was doing okay. People either loved or hated him with a passion. Daily, 5,000 to 8,000 letters, many warmly personal, came flooding into the White House, a tenfold increase over Hoover days. To the little people who wrote these letters, Roosevelt was a personal savior. On the other hand, more prosperous citizens saw Roosevelt as the very devil, and the nation's press, 85 per cent anti-F.D.R., went to absurd lengths to hand the devil what-for. Switchboard operators at the Chicago *Tribune* answered phones before the 1936 election with an ominous: "Do you know there are only -- days to save your country?"

Love him or hate him, the nation was more aware of F.D.R. than of any previous President. This awareness is reflected in the letters excerpted below from the White House mail bag and in the newspaper columns and editorials at right. Some of these anti-F.D.R. comments were pretty rough. A Westbrook Pegler column made Roosevelt's sons so angry they planned literally to horsewhip Pegler until their father calmly talked them out of it. When F.D.R. got their grudging promise to desist, he laughed, saying: "Not that it isn't a grand idea—'in principle'!"

Dear Mr. President:

This is just to tell you that everything is all right now. The man you sent found our house all right, and we went down to the bank with him and the mortgage can go on for a while longer. You remember I wrote you about losing the furniture too. Well, your man got it back for us. I never heard of a President like you.

My dear sir,

It is expensive and a headache to have a playboy as President. Wipe that grin off your face.

Dear President Roosevelt:

I'm proud of our United States and every time I hear the "Star-Spangled Banner" I feel a lump in my throat. There ain't no other nation in the world that would have sense enough to think of WPA and all the other A's.

Mr. President:

If you could get around the country as I have and seen the distress forced upon the American people, you would throw your damn NRA and AAA, and every other God-Damn A into the sea, before you and your crooked crowd are taken out as they are in Germany, and that is just what you and the rest deserve. You are not for the poor nor the middle class, but for the rich, the monopolies, Jewry, and perhaps Communism.

Dear Honored Mr. Roosevelt:

I never saw a President I would write to until youve got in your place, but I have always felt like you and your wife and your children were as common as we were.

Dear Pres. Roosevelt

How's our dandy little quarterback tonight? Our little "planner that wayer", eh? What's become of the "happy days are here again" boys? F. Depression Roosevelt. They tell me that you have no brains or mind of your own—that you are just a "Charlie McCarthy" for a couple of smarties called Cohen and Corcoran or Kelly or something. That's a terrible blow—to find out that our big, noble savior of the common peepul is nothing but a stooge.

The Chief instructs that the phrase Soak the Successful be used in all references to the Administration's tax program instead of the phrase Soak the Thrifty hitherto used, also he wants the words Raw Deal used instead of New Deal.

EXECUTIVE DICTUM TO HEARST EDITORS, 1935

New York, Oct. 28.—Confidence that President Roosevelt will be reelected pervades the headquarters of the communist party. Based on that confidence is the high optimism of communist leaders that another four years of the New Deal will bring them within striking distance of the overthrow of the American form of government and the substitution therefor of a communist state.

ARTHUR SEARS HENNING, CHICAGO TRIBUNE, OCTOBER 29, 1936

Mr. Roosevelt himself never spent a day in a public school in all his life. When Mr. Roosevelt had done with nurse and tutors he went to a dude school named Groton, which prepared him for Harvard, and after he had married and taken his bride for a honeymoon tour of England, France, Italy and Germany they returned home for him to go to Columbia Law School. "My mother-in-law," writes Mrs. Roosevelt in her book, "had taken a home for us. She had furnished it and engaged our servants. In summer we visited my mother-in-law at Hyde Park for a time and then went up to stay with her at Campobello. My husband sailed up and down the coast in the little schooner 'Half Moon' and took short cruises." In 1908 the President's mother thought their little house too small and therefore bought a plot in New York and built another for them. Later she also gave to Franklin Roosevelt and his young wife an estate on Campobello Island.

For Mr. Roosevelt to sail his own schooner around Fundy when he had never yet assumed the task of supporting his own wife unassisted was all right, but let some other man cock a funny cap over his eye and toss off such words as "Ahoy!" "Port!" and "Starboard!" on a yacht bought with his own money in enjoyment of his own success and he is not merely ridiculous but an enemy of the great common people of whom the President is paradoxically one. There are those who called Mr. Roosevelt a traitor to his class, but that cry comes from the hereditary rich who grew up endowed and, as he did, looked to their mothers and fathers for support and luxuries long after they had ceased to be children. The class that I have in mind are proud to have taken care of their own parents, and every crack from him about well-fed clubmen and economic royalists evokes from them the soul-satisfying and contemptuous taunt, "mama's boy."

THE DISSENTING OPINIONS OF MISTER WESTBROOK PEGLER, 1938

If the New Deal goes on to the only destination it can have, this may be the last presidential election America will have. It is tragic that America fails to see that the New Deal is to America what the early phase of Nazism was to Germany and the early phase of Fascism to Italy.

MARK SULLIVAN, BUFFALO EVENING NEWS, NOVEMBER 16, 1935

The President of the United States has smeared businessmen. His smearing of the newspapers has become one of his confirmed habits, joyously adopted by the radicals in the Cabinet and the pinks among the White House intimates. We have seen the Administration smear the doctors and we have seen it smear the lawyers. There has been a flood of smearing books, ranging from economic volumes revealing the iniquities of our alleged "ruling families" to exaggerated novels calculated to stir the emotions of uninformed and credulous people. The whole smearing game seems to have become a more or less deliberate attempt to destroy respect for the social order and faith in the American economic system by untruth, half-truth and misrepresentation.

FRANK R. KENT, BALTIMORE SUN, AUGUST 24, 1939

"*Come·along. We're going to the Trans-Lux to hiss Roosevelt.*"

While some of the anti-F.D.R. talk was vicious, most of the protests over the President were reasonably mild and sort of funny. One thing that made them funny was that they erupted among such dignified, genteel people. The mood of disapproval among the gentility was caught beautifully by the *New Yorker* magazine both in Peter Arno's cartoon *(left)* and in humorist Frank Sullivan's compilation *(excerpted below)* of polite anti-F.D.R. jargon as delivered by one Mr. Arbuthnot, the Cliché Expert. Note: Mr. Arbuthnot was imaginary, but his clichés were not.

Mr. *Arbuthnot: No sir! Nobody is going to tell ME how to run my business.*

Q: *Mr. Arbuthnot, you sound like a Roosevelt hater.*

A: *I certainly am.*

Q: *Perhaps you could give us an idea of some of the clichés your set is in the habit of using in speaking of Mr. Roosevelt. . . .*

A: *Well, we call him That Madman in the White House, or That Fellow Down in Washington. Sometimes we call him MISTER Roosevelt, or Your FRIEND, Franklin D.—like that.*

Q: *Sort of sarcastic, eh?*

A: *And how! Now don't misunderstand me. I'm a liberal. I'm in favor of a lot of the reforms Roosevelt has been trying to put over, but I don't like the way he's going about it.*

Q: *For instance?*

A: *Well, you take the Supreme Court. Where Roosevelt made his big mistake was in attacking the Court.*

Q: *I see.*

A: *And where Roosevelt made his big mistake was in arousing all this class hatred. You know, all this forgotten-man stuff.*

Q: *Yes.*

A: *And where Roosevelt made his big mistake was in all this pump priming. You can't spend your way out of a depression.*

Q: *Really?*

A: *Certainly not. Where's the money coming from to pay for all this—this—*

Q: *Do you mean "orgy of spending"?*

A: *That's just the phrase I was searching for.*

Q: *What about the WPA, Mr. Arbuthnot?*

A: *Oh, the shovel brigade. I'm against the WPA and all this alphabet-soup stuff. Say, did you hear about the WPA worker and King Solomon? Why is a WPA worker like King Solomon?*

Q: *I heard it. Now then—*

A: *Because he takes his pick and goes to bed. . . .*

Q: *Mr. Arbuthnot, you slay me. Well, go on. Tell us more.*

A: *Well, the trouble with Roosevelt is he's an idealist.*

Q: *Yes?*

A: *And the trouble is he's destroyed individual initiative.*

Q: *Do tell.*

A: *And he's a Communist.*

Q: *I see. Go on.*

A: *The trouble with Roosevelt is he's a Fascist.*

Q: *A Fascist, too?*

A: *Certainly. He wants to be a dictator.*

Q: *Mr. Arbuthnot, your comments have been confined to Mr. Roosevelt's policies. Have you, as an expert in the jargon of the Roosevelt haters, anything to say about his personal life?*

A: *Have I? Oh boy! Why, he's a rich man's son. He never did a tap of work in his life. Where does HE get off, posing as a champion of the people?*

Q: *A traitor to his class, eh?*

A: *Oh, we don't use that chestnut any more. It's out of date.*

FRANK SULLIVAN IN *THE NEW YORKER* MAGAZINE, JUNE 18, 1938

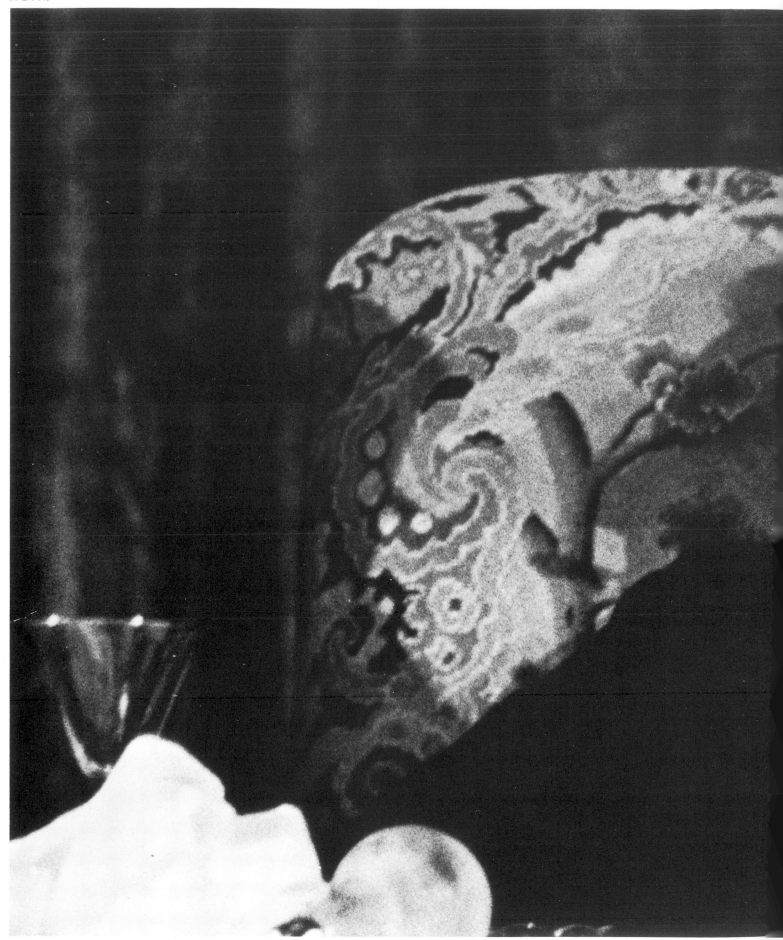

Undismayed by his critics, a relaxed F.D.R. radiates confidence. "He must have been psychoanalyzed by God," declared an awed associate.

Café Society

A Conga line snakes through revelers at New York's Rainbow Room.

Something Old, Something New

I'm established now for '38

With the title of glamor and reprobate.

I've won a position in Vogue and Harper's;

For a hundred bucks I'll advertise garters.

I grit my teeth and smile at my enemies;

I sit at the Stork Club and talk to nonentities.

"GLAMOR GIRL SERENADE" BY BRENDA FRAZIER, 1938

When most of the country hit rock bottom, old-fashioned High Society foundered along with it. Out of the rubble of Newport and Fifth Avenue, however, emerged some survivors who joined a pack of movie stars and gossip columnists and various hangers-on to create something new: a glittering, publicity-mad, indefatigable set called "Café Society." The "cafés" where this group sported were the old speak-easies, which after Prohibition was repealed in 1933 were reborn as chic restaurants: New York's Stork Club, El Morocco, "21," and the like.

The queen of the new gentlefolk was Brenda Frazier, heiress granddaughter of social arbiter Lady Williams-Taylor and so-called Glamor Girl of 1938. On any given night Brenda might be seen dining with her latest beau at the Colony. On such an evening, the table next to Brenda's would be presided over by someone like Grand Duchess Marie, cousin to Russia's last czar and now a commercial photographer. The Duchess, a formidable presence in her own right, usually appeared with a clutch of other deposed Europeans: Prince Serge Obolensky, who ran a restaurant at the St. Regis Hotel; and Princess Ketto Mikeladze, the negligée buyer at Elizabeth Arden's. Occasionally the expatriate crowd would admit into their presence their dear friend, red-hot mama Sophie Tucker.

Such egalitarianism was typical of the new free-for-all, in which Astors, Vanderbilts and Whitneys mixed with popular entertainers, while English titleholders sipped cocktails with advertising executives. Marrying and divorcing were equally indiscriminate: women bore names such as "Mrs. Margaret Emerson-McKim-Vanderbilt-Baker-Amory-Emerson" and "Mrs. Millicent Rogers-Salm-Hoogstraetan-Ramos-Balcom."

The ring-mistress of it all was Elsa Maxwell, a fat nobody from Keokuk, Iowa, who had somehow managed to meet *everybody*. She was also quite adroit at getting instant publicity for favored friends. Thus a socially ambitious new woman in town would wangle an invitation to one of Elsa's bashes. And if that same woman had a good press agent, she might finally win one of Café Society's ultimate accolades—her picture in the new picture magazine LIFE with a caption like the following classic tribute to conspicuous inconsequence: "Mrs. Orson D. Munn, who won fame in a limited circle by wearing a foxtail for a hat at the Colony Restaurant, drops in at El Morocco several times a week, is known for the spirited way she dances the rumba with her remarkably agile husband."

Shouting "Oy!" two dancers do the final step of the Lambeth Walk, which originated in England in 1938 and was adopted by Americans.

Sheathed in satin, Brenda Frazier models the gown she wore to her debut. The party made nationwide news; one paper crowed, "Bow's A Wow."

The Ultimate Glamor Girl

The fame of the stars of Café Society went far beyond their own set; at 17, Brenda Frazier was one of the most celebrated personalities in the whole country. Miss Frazier modestly pretended to be astonished by the big fuss: "I don't deserve all this. I haven't done anything at all. I'm just a debutante."

It was true. She hadn't done a thing—except dance every night till five in the morning with scores of men, including Bruce Cabot and Douglas Fairbanks Jr., and pose at the flash of a bulb for any photographer in sight.

Brenda epitomized the Glamor Girl, the idealized woman of the decade. Her extraordinarily pale skin contrasted sharply with her vermilion lipstick, black hair and pencilled eyebrows. She also made the strapless evening gown (*page 150*) a national fad. Although she was due to inherit four million dollars when she was 21, Brenda found it fun to pose for Woodbury Soap ads.

During her big year as 1938's No. 1 Glamor Girl, Brenda worked on 15 charity committees and served as the chairman of an enormous bash called the Velvet Ball. The high point of her brief and spectacular career, however, was really its beginning, her own debut. The description below of that Keystone Kops affair is excerpted from a *New Yorker* profile of Brenda that appeared in June 1939.

The theoretic climax of any debutante's season is her own coming-out party. Brenda happened to have a cold at the time, and the tabloids reported this with all the gravity that might attend the last earthly hours of a dying king or queen. Brenda's ball at the Ritz, despite her indisposition, was a gala affair, disturbed only by uninvited cameramen. Mrs. Watriss [her mother], who had decided that on this one night at least Brenda should remain pictorially unchronicled in the press, barred all photographers but Jay Te Winburn, who was commissioned to record the occasion for Brenda's future entertainment. This was an admirable idea, but Mrs. Watriss underestimated the resourcefulness of the "Daily News," which dressed half a dozen men in tailcoats and supplied them with a room in the Ritz. From there they drifted casually into the ballroom, armed with concealed candid cameras. One, who decided that the chances of taking his own shots without being observed would be slim, sneaked up behind Mr. Winburn and, every time that fast-working gentleman laid down an exposed plate to pick up a fresh one, slipped it under his coat. After a spell he strolled out and sent his collection to the "News." Another stationed himself on the bandstand, disguised as a musician. While waiting for an opportunity to begin shooting, however, he was recognized by another jealous photographer, a Russian free-lancer, who had managed to get in, but without his camera. The Russian reported the presence of the "News" man to Brenda, who had him thrown out and then had the Russian thrown out too. She just stared blankly at one "News" man who was making faces at her to hold her attention. She took him for one of the thousand guests. By the time the last edition of the "News" went to press, the whole story was ready in pictures—including Brenda being, so the caption read, kissed by an anonymous admirer. Reporters grew hysterical over the food, the music, and the cost (which was reported to have been as high as $60,000), and Elsa Maxwell complained subsequently that she hadn't been able to get a chicken sandwich. The only missing detail was: Who had kissed Brenda? The "News" didn't know, and neither did a society press agent whom the paper called in. Brenda refused to say who he was and maintained that he had only been whispering. That remark got no more attention than Mrs. Watriss's anguished statement, printed in subsequent editions, that the party had cost just under $16,000—which, as deb parties have gone, is neither little nor much. —E. J. KAHN JR. IN *THE NEW YORKER*, JUNE 9, 1939

A Mother's Pride

"Certainly in 1939 Cobina, Jr. was the 'most' girl, most photographed,
most publicized, most sought after," announced her mother,
Cobina Wright Sr. To make sure it all kept happening, Mrs. Wright arranged
a screen test for Cobina Jr., hurled the girl into the
unreceptive arms of Britain's Prince Philip and eventually ended up
singing duets with her daughter in a nightclub (both wore Daniel Boone hats).

A Precocious Spender

One of the gayest Glamor Girls was Gloria (Mimi) Baker, who came
out in 1937. Ravishingly pretty, by the time she was 15
she had become a habitual nightclubber and frequenter of gambling casinos.
Her debut was so ostentatious that even gossip columnists
condemned her as a decadent aristocrat; her mother denied the charge, saying
that Mimi was "the most democratic person, bar none, I've ever known."

Debs on the Go

Wherever Brenda, Cobina and Mimi went, whomever they married,
whatever they wore, received instant fame. In fact, these
"celebutantes," as Walter Winchell called them, were such sure-fire publicity
getters that nightclubs sometimes wooed them by giving them the
best tables closest to the action and charging them only a dollar for dinner.

In her trend-setting strapless, Brenda Frazier leads the Grand March at the Velvet Ball. At age 14 her clothing allowance was $5,400 a year.

Brenda goes out with an Indian prince. . .   chats with Bill DeRham, a dance instructor. . .   and registers joy at a witty remark.

Cobina Wright Jr. steals a march in Florida by dating Julian Gerard, one of Brenda's beaux.

Cesar Romero ogles Cobina at a premiere.

Mimi Baker wows 'em with "crazyjamas."

Alfred G. Vanderbilt gives away his half-sister Mimi to New York socialite Bob Topping.

Mimi dates the elusive Howard Hughes.

With suave smile and drooping lids, Alfred G. Vanderbilt dances with film star Joan Crawford at the 1937 Screen Actors Guild Ball in Los Angeles.

A light drinker, Vanderbilt has a Coke with starlet K. T. Stevens.

His Saratoga visit with divorced star Joan Bennett stirs gossip.

Alfred dates actress known as Margo . . .   pretty torch singer Gertrude Niesen . . .   and Manhattan deb Eleanor Young.

Prince of the Glamor Boys

The male counterpart to the Glamor Girl in Café Society was the Man About Town, and for several seasons Alfred Gwynne Vanderbilt led the pack. He had all the qualifications. He was young and handsome, possessed an old name and had inherited millions. When he was 21 (in 1933) he had also inherited his mother's racing stable, Sagamore Farm, and in 1936 his horses earned more money than those of any other American sportsman. As if all those qualifications weren't enough, Alf had as his half-sister Glamor Girl Mimi Baker. Moreover, he had been elected best-dressed man in America by a group of tailors and he was very clever at holding the tablecloth when Ernest Hemingway wanted to play bull to Alf's *torero*. Almost every night he could be seen night-clubbing with a different Glamor Girl or movie star and he never shooed photographers away or bothered to deny gossip columnist rumors that a "romance was brewing." Then, in 1938, he climaxed his gay career as glamor boy and brought an end to all the romantic rumors by marrying another wealthy race-track addict, Manuela (Molly) Hudson.

The Queen from Keokuk

"My social whirl was purely a labor of love in pursuit of pleasure," Elsa Maxwell once announced. Into that pursuit, she poured all her immense energies—disdaining sexual ones. "I wouldn't subject myself to it," she told an interviewer. "I married the world—the world is my husband. That is why I'm so young. No sex. Sex is the most tiring thing in the world."

Elsa was famous for her lavish parties, such as her Pet Hates Ball to which everyone came as his bête noire (she had to limit the number of Franklin and Eleanor Roosevelts). In 1938 Elsa described to gossip columnist Inez Robb the assets she expected of all guests at her parties.

First, I want a woman guest to be beautiful. Second, I want her to be beautifully dressed. Third, I demand animation and vivacity. Fourth, not too many brains. Brains are always awkward at a gay and festive party. Brains are only a requisite when the party is limited to a handful of persons, say six or eight.

And fifth, I expect obedience. It's ruinous if guests refuse to cooperate with a hostess if she asks them to dance, play games, go on a treasure hunt, tell stories, guess riddles or whatever she has planned for the occasion.

Above all things, a man should be good-looking. Then he should boast a tailor who is an artist. Third, he must not be overly married. This is a matter of attitude, which has nothing to do with the fidelity to the wife of his bosom, but with a willingness to make himself charming and a bit flattering to other women.

Fourth, men guests must not only dance well but be willing to dance. You've no idea what a problem that is. Finally, all men should have manner and manners. I want them to reply to invitations which they receive and I don't want them to carry the champagne home under their coats instead of their belts, and I'd rather they didn't throw bottles out of the window.

THE NEW YORK MIRROR, DECEMBER 16, 1938

Elsa toasts suave William Rhinelander Stewart (left) and composer Cole Porter. Porter and Aly Khan were the two men Elsa considered sexy.

Barbara Hutton in 1930

Poor Little Rich Girl

The star-crossed darling of Café Society was Barbara Hutton, an heiress to a $45 million share of the Woolworth fortune. When she was 13, she wrote prophetically: "Why should some have all / And others be without? / Why should men pretend / And women have to doubt?"

The first man to pretend he loved Barbara, and whom she learned to doubt too late, was a self-styled Russian prince, Alexis Mdivani. Mdivani first met Barbara on the Riviera when she was a fat, homely teenager. Although he was honeymooning with his first bride, American heiress Louise Van Alen, Mdivani made a beeline for Barbara and chatted with her all afternoon.

After restraining himself for all of three years while Barbara grew up a little, Mdivani demanded and got a million-dollar settlement out of his first wife. Then the good Prince Alexis moved in for the kill. Barbara's thoroughly alarmed father spirited her off on a world tour; but the intrepid Mdivani pursued her to Bangkok, and in a few weeks the happy couple announced their engagement.

The wedding took place in Paris. Barbara presented the Prince with a string of polo ponies and the Prince presented Barbara with a string of jade beads, which she paid for. Barbara's father gave the groom a token million and the newlyweds took off for India. Soon after the honeymoon, however, Mdivani was reported to have screamed at Barbara, "You're as fat as a pig," and to be devoting most of his time to women more svelte. Barbara endured

1933. Barbara Hutton marries Prince Mdivani in Paris.

1934. Barbara returns to America dieted down 44 pounds.

1935. She marries Count von Haugwitz-Reventlow.

1936. Kurt, Barbara baptize their son Lance in London.

1937. Barbara and Kurt (left) admit they will split.

Barbara Hutton in 1940

two subsequent years of neglect and strenuous dieting, but then called it quits and gave Mdivani another two million toward settlement.

A new European aristocrat was lying in wait, Count Kurt von Haugwitz-Reventlow, and the day after she had stopped being a Georgian princess, Barbara became a Danish countess. "Now at last I have found happiness," Barbara announced. "My search is ended. I know that this is safe and sure." Safe and sure it wasn't, but Bar-

---

In a foreign land is a very young woman—only 26—who has had a strange life. She is alone, attacked by her husband. She's an American girl fighting alone across the sea. She's made mistakes, been a silly, wild, foolish girl, given in to temptations— but she's still our own. COLUMNIST ADELA ROGERS ST. JOHNS, 1938.

---

bara spared no expense in trying to make it so. For one thing, she shelled out $4.5 million building a huge mansion in London. During her stay in England, Barbara gave birth to her only child, Lance. A year later, in 1937, the marriage was on the rocks and Barbara commented: "Poor Kurt, I feel sorry for him. It was always, 'I am Count von Haugwitz-Reventlow.' He never forgot it—until one day I said, 'Who cares? Who cares about the Count von Haugwitz-Reventlow today? The world has come a long way from that sort of thing.'"

The world had also come a long way from admiring flighty heiresses. In 1939, when Barbara returned to the U.S., Woolworth clerks picketed her hotel and crowds threatened her. "Why do they hate me?" Barbara asked. "There are other girls as rich, richer, almost as rich."

Sensationally bored and cut off from the world by a gold chain, two girls of Café Society sit it out at a supper club with their equally glum escort.

Labor

Cleveland cops move in as strikers overturn a foreman's car.

The Worker Finds a Voice

Labor, like Israel, has many sorrows. Its women keep their fallen and they lament for the future of the children of the race.

JOHN L. LEWIS

By the middle of the 1930s the American workingman was stalking toward a deadly showdown with management. Thanks largely to the shrewd lobbying of bushy-browed John L. Lewis, formidable leader of the United Mine Workers, a federal law was on the books guaranteeing every laborer the right to join a union and use the union to bargain with his bosses. But acknowledging labor's rights by law was easier said than done. In many a big industrial town the only real law was the company's.

In those harsh times, firing was about the mildest punishment given a union organizer. A fair number of U.S. laborers actually worked at gunpoint. Why, a Senate committee had wanted to know in 1928, did the Pittsburgh Coal Company keep machine guns at its coal pits? "You cannot run the mines without them," replied Richard B. Mellon, chairman of the board. In 1935 hired guns still loomed over the toughest of the company towns, where a word for the union could get a man beaten up or killed.

When a strike was brewing in 1935 against the Akron, Ohio, tire manufacturers, the rubber companies had an army of strikebreakers standing by under the direction of one Pearl Bergoff, a king among strikebreakers. Pearl's delicate name mocked his nature (his mother gave him

the name she had picked for the daughter she wanted to have). He ran a multi-million-dollar business, serving various major firms across the country, from an office in New York. His aides daily scanned out-of-town newspapers for hints of brewing strikes, whereupon Pearl dispatched one of his salesmen to peddle the Bergoff services. The deal included shipping a small army of men to fill the struck jobs and fitting them out with weapons from Pearl's armory of machine guns, night sticks and tear gas.

Bergoff was not the only big-time goon for hire. The Pinkerton National Detective Agency, a favorite of the auto companies, earned $1,750,000 for its services to industry between 1933 and 1936. "We must do it," explained Vice President Herman L. Weckler of the Chrysler Corporation, "to obtain the information we need in dealing with our employees." By the mid '30s, however, industrial employees all over the country had long since become fed up with such dealing. And they were rallying behind John L. Lewis, whose tough leadership and political power had brought a new era into view.

They could hardly have had a better man. Lewis had been in the thick of union wars for 25 years. As a teenager with a seventh-grade education, he had gone to work

In 1936, labor czar John L. Lewis blasts Republican Presidential candidate Alf Landon as a "pitiful puppet responsible to the steel industry."

in the coal pits of Iowa with his five kid brothers. His awesome energies, angry convictions and eloquent tongue soon won him a niche of his own in the United Mine Workers. A six-foot-three-inch bull of a man, Lewis had a mind as powerful as his imposing physique. At night and on union organizing trips across the country, he read in their entirety the Bible, the Odyssey and the Iliad, Oswald Spengler and Shakespeare, Karl Marx and Friedrich Engels. By early 1934 this unique mixture of coal miner, labor organizer and reader of classics was entrenched as president of the UMW, and with the backing of the new federal law, he had built the union to 400,000 members and taken the field against intransigent mine owners of Pennsylvania in the first of the decade's climactic labor wars. This occurred in midsummer of 1934, when Lewis called out 70,000 miners to strike.

The companies and their political allies girded for battle. "We're going to meet 'em at the bridge and break their goddam heads," shouted the mayor of Duquesne as the strike spread across the Allegheny Valley. Before it ended, the mine owners had poured some $17,000 into munitions and their henchmen had bombed miners' houses and set crosses ablaze on the hillsides. But in the set-

---

So I'm a Red? I suppose it makes me a Red because I don't like making time so hard on these goddamned machines. When I get home I'm so tired I can't sleep with my wife.

ASSEMBLY-LINE WORKER, 1935

---

tlement, the embattled miners won grudging acceptance, and the road toward union recognition was staked out for every man in America's far-flung laboring forces.

With this triumph under his belt, Lewis met with union organizers in Atlantic City, New Jersey, and proposed a drive to pull together all of the country's industrial laborers into an enormous conglomerate. At one point in the maneuvering, Lewis was challenged by a burly trade unionist who called Lewis a "big bastard," to which Lewis replied with a punch in the nose. When the dust of the skirmish had cleared away, a good many of labor's top

THEY SHALL NOT PASS

Armed with billy clubs and auto parts, Chrysler strikers rally beneath a slogan—borrowed from French soldiers—warning scabs to stay away.

Sit-down strikers take it easy on assembly-line auto seats inside besieged Fisher Body plant in Flint, Michigan, during the crucial strike of 1937.

men had fallen in behind Lewis; the labor conglomerate was formed and subsequently christened the Congress of Industrial Organizations, the CIO. Looking back with a certain pleasure on the imbroglios involved, Lewis crowed: "They smote me hip and thigh, and right merrily did I return their blows."

Then he returned to the war with industrial management, this time in Flint, Michigan, home of several General Motors plants. General Motors was then the third largest corporation in the country. It employed a quarter of a million people, paying its top 20 officials an average of $200,000, its workers scarcely $1,000. It also maintained one of the rankest spy systems in the country; between January 1934 and August 1936 the company paid $994,855.68 to Pinkerton and others.

On December 28, 1936, a thousand workers at one of GM's Cleveland plants, demanding the right to make every GM worker a member of the United Auto Workers, adopted a somewhat new and disconcertingly effective tactic. They laid down their tools and went on a sit-down strike; instead of walking out, as most earlier strikers had done, they remained in the plant. Management was stunned. Two days later the night shift at GM's key Chevrolet plant in Flint sat down too. Fifteen more plants followed, stripping General Motors of 140,000 employees, and bringing all auto production to a halt.

The focal point of the conflict was at Flint. As the sit-down continued, the temperature dropped below zero, and General Motors officials turned off the heat in the plant and directed the Flint police to seize food bound for the shivering strikers. Some 50 policemen sprayed the pickets with buckshot and tear gas and beat them with clubs. "We wanted peace. General Motors chose war. Give it to them!" shouted a voice over a loudspeaker, and the strikers did, with pipes, door hinges, coffee mugs, pop bottles, and an icy blast from the company's fire hose. After an all-night battle in which 14 men were wounded, the strikers succeeded in routing the police.

Governor Frank Murphy, who had given grueling hours to patient mediation and was determined to keep Mich-

Ford goons stalk unionists Walter Reuther, Richard Frankensteen.

Grabbing Frankensteen, they slug him for handing out union leaflets.

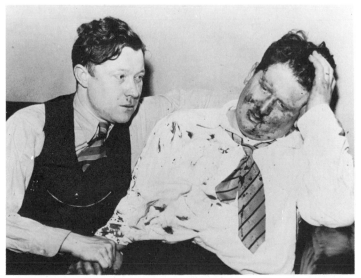

After the brawl, Reuther attempts to comfort the bloodied Frankensteen.

As news of the strikers' victory comes, a jubilant Ladies Auxiliary parades in front of the Chrysler works just before the sit-downers emerge.

igan from further bloodshed, alerted the National Guard. But he decided to consult with Lewis before sending the men into action. What would Lewis do if the Guard tried to evict the strikers, Murphy wanted to know.

"You want my answer, sir?" asked Lewis. "I give it to you. Tomorrow morning, I shall personally enter General Motors plant Chevrolet No. 4. I shall order the men to disregard your order. I shall then walk up to the largest window in the plant, open it, divest myself of my outer raiment, remove my shirt and bare my bosom. Then when you order your troops to fire, mine will be the first those bullets will strike. And as my body falls from that window to the ground, you listen to the voice of your grandfather as he whispers in your ear, 'Frank, are you sure you are doing the right thing?' " Murphy, whose grandfather had been hanged in the Irish rebellion, blanched and tore up his order. He further forbade General Motors to bar the delivery of food to the strikers and with great tact held further violence at bay.

After 44 days of losing profits at the rate of one million dollars a day, General Motors capitulated, agreeing to bargain with the United Automobile Workers in the 17 plants that had been struck. In four months' time the U.A.W. had won its drive for acceptance and organized a majority of General Motors workers. The strikers had scored a monumental triumph against the third mightiest corporation in the country. In the wake of that victory labor's final battles for union recognition got under way (*pages 172-177*).

When they tie the can to a union man,
 Sit down! Sit down!
When they give him the sack they'll take him back,
 Sit down! Sit down!
When the speed-up comes, just twiddle your thumbs,
 Sit down! Sit down!
When the boss won't talk, don't take a walk,
 Sit down! Sit down!

      UNION BALLAD

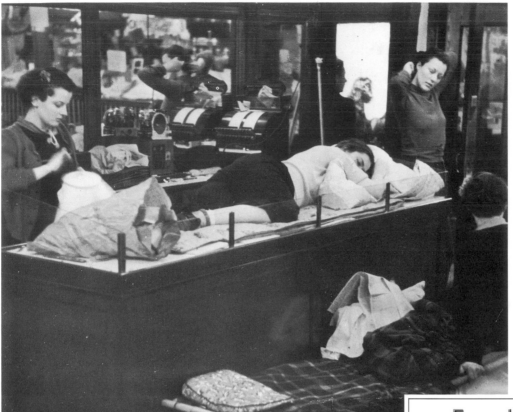

Woolworth clerk naps on a counter during a sit-in at Detroit in 1937.

Everybody Sits

With the success of the big strikes, people all over sat down to protest grievances.

Striking chefs at the Willard Hotel in Washington, D.C., stage their sit-down on top of a cold stove.

An Illinois driver demands the road be f...

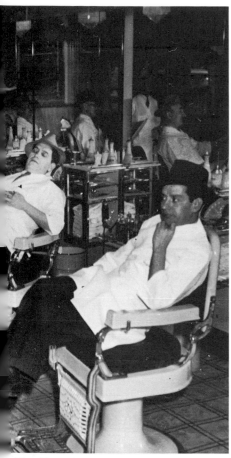

New Jersey barbers sit in a non-union shop.

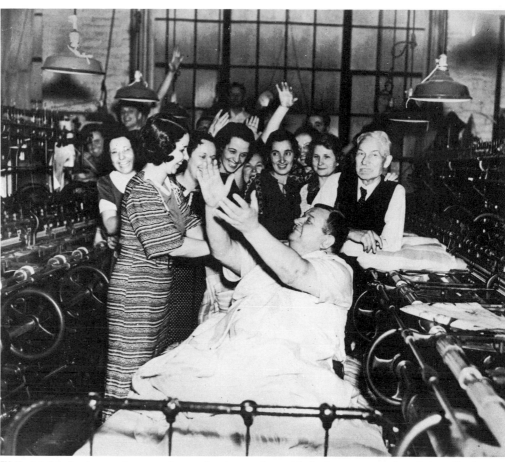

Philadelphia hosiery makers awaken a sleeping worker with the happy news that their strike is won.

ve been stuck here 32 times," he declared.

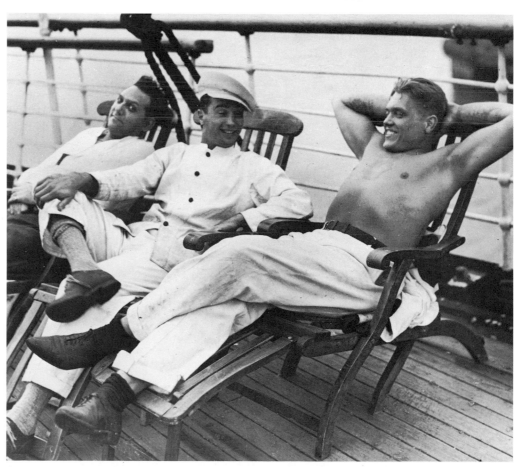

Striking seamen lounge in deck chairs aboard the S.S. "President Roosevelt" en route to Hamburg.

The Hard Grip of Steel

While the nation's eyes were still fixed on the union coup in the automobile industry at Detroit, labor's eloquent leader, John L. Lewis, got busy elsewhere. He took on, virtually singlehanded, the Goliath of American industry: United States Steel, an antagonist beside which even General Motors seemed comparatively small.

Despite the hard times of the Depression, U.S. Steel, grandly called The Corporation by its officers, reported gross earnings of $35,218,359 in 1934. It turned out more than 53 million tons of iron ore, coal, coke, limestone, pig iron, ingots and finished steel items, and more than a quarter of a million tons of by-products from ammonia to cement. It owned not only mills, but coal and iron mines stretching from Canada to Brazil, a fleet of ships and miles of railroad tracks to move its cargo.

But the view from inside the mills and mines, the view of the common laborer, was grim and hopeless. In 1933, more than half the mill hands were totally unemployed, and by The Corporation's own statement there was not a single full-time worker anywhere on its payroll. Condi-

A world without policemen would be like a world without music.
DANIEL J. SHIELDS, MAYOR OF JOHNSTOWN, PENNSYLVANIA

tions elsewhere in the steel industry were much the same. That year the average steelworker, with his part-time pickings, earned $369, a sum on which he had to support a family that averaged 5.92 persons. "Work two days a week," said a steelworker in Braddock, Pennsylvania, "loaf around five days, wife sick, one of my girls needs a good doctor, and me with no money, a bunch of rent bills, butcher bills, grocery bills."

Safety conditions were as bad as wages. Occupational diseases such as carbon monoxide poisoning, "hot mill cramps" (from exposure to temperatures up to 220° F. at the furnace mouth) and pneumonia took hundreds of lives every year. Every week, on the average, one man could expect his clothes to catch fire, and if he did not burn to death he had to replace the clothes from his meager earnings. The overseer who went by the title of safety manager at a Jones & Laughlin steel mill in Pittsburgh admitted

to having "a lot of equipment that is out of date, lacks the new safety devices and is liable to break down at any time, causing serious accidents," but he had no plans for improving it. "It still yields a return on investment," he said, "so the company cannot scrap it." Instead the industry scrapped 22,845 human beings in accidents in a single year: 242 were killed, 1,193 permanently disabled and 21,410 temporarily laid up.

As top dog in the industry, U.S. Steel was habitually followed by its pack of friendly competitors in all matters from wage rates to safety measures and, of course, in its attitude toward unions. On that score, Bethlehem, Republic, Youngstown, National and Inland—nicknamed "Little Steel" to differentiate them from the grandiose Corporation—shot down unions with a vigor that would have warmed the hearts of the tough old magnates who laid the foundations of U.S. Steel.

In 1935 Carnegie Steel was paying likely finks about $25 a month to report on union talk among their fellow workers, filing the results of their pickings and firing offenders. Yet Tom M. Girdler, one-time policeman for Jones & Laughlin, now head of Republic Steel, could accuse union organizers of "interference in a man's private affairs." He added: "An ominous fact was repeated in the sketchy facts we had about some of these fellows: They were Communists."

There were some unions in the steel industry, but they were company unions, organizations controlled not by the workers but by management. A Ukrainian mill hand testified at a government investigation of the company union at the Carnegie Steel plant in Duquesne: "Boss say, 'Better you go vote now.' No, I say, I got outside union. I vote in outside union. Boss say then, 'You no like job, huh? No like company? Well, maybe company no like you. Better you go vote now.' "

In all, the steelworkers seemed helpless to improve their lot. But the momentum of the big union victories in coal and autos provided fresh hope; and help was on the way as John L. Lewis, now head of the CIO, stepped forward as the steelworkers' spokesman. By organizing coal,

Cartoonist William Gropper bitterly caricatured the repressions of the Chicago steel magnates against workers who struck in the spring of 1937.

A fallen worker gets a merciless beating as strikers fight scabs during a 1937 strike at Republic Steel in Cleveland. Eighteen workers lost their lives.

he had tied up the source of the fuel on which the steel industry ran; by organizing automobiles, he had tied up steel's major customer. Now he turned to U.S. Steel, certain that if he could move the mighty Corporation its confreres in Little Steel would come along. "If we can organize here," he said, "the rest will follow. If the crouching lion can be routed, it is a safe bet that the hyenas in the adjacent bush may be scattered along the plain."

John L. Lewis was, as a reporter of the day remarked, "a foeman worthy of U.S. Steel." Calling personally on Myron Taylor, the courtly board chairman of The Corporation, he chatted amiably of Gothic tapestries and high finance. Taylor was charmed, and to the nation's astonishment, he signed a contract with the CIO union. After 50 years of losing to clubs and gunfire, the steelworkers

Strikers support a tear-gassed co-worker.

seemed to have won the war with Lewis' mellifluous words.

Unhappily, peace in the industry was still some distance away, for the "hyenas in the adjacent bush" were not so easily scattered. Two months after the U.S. Steel settlement, Little Steel had not budged toward any settlement with the CIO. On May 26, seventy thousand workers walked out of 27 plants belonging to Little Steel in seven states, and the companies countered with the bloodiest anti-union battle of the decade.

On Memorial Day some 1,500 workers with their wives and children gathered for a demonstration of solidarity outside the Republic plant in South Chicago. "CIO! Let's go! CIO! Let's go!" they chanted. A corps of 150 Chicago police stormed them with tear gas, night sticks and 200 rounds of gunfire. "Stand back, you son of a bitch," said one of the cops, "or I will fill you full of lead." Over the next

---

Give me 200 good, tough armed men and I'll clean up them sons of bitches on the picket line.

DISTRICT ATTORNEY, YOUNGSTOWN, OHIO

---

few minutes, in a bloodbath that came to be called the Memorial Day Massacre, the police killed 10 demonstrators and wounded more than 100 others.

"There can be no pity for a mob," said Republic president Tom M. Girdler later, as if to excuse the violence. "As that artistic brawler, Benvenuto Cellini, said," he went on, " 'blows are not dealt by measure.' Some of the mob were clubbed after they had started to run from the wrath they had aroused. Some women were knocked down. The policemen were there performing a hazardous and harsh duty. What were women doing there?"

The Little Steel strike lasted two months, and this time the laborers lost. Vigilantes lined up against the strikers; the National Guard was called in to back up management; and the various companies in Little Steel maintained a united front. The workers were up against too much. Exhausted and hungry, they went back to work in July without winning their union.

The loss of the Little Steel strike was a bitter blow to workers everywhere after the heady victories that had

gone before it. But it proved to be only a temporary setback. Senator Robert M. La Follette Jr. of Wisconsin launched investigations that exposed the tactics used to crush the Little Steel strike and others, with the result that public opinion began to change and industrial espionage and the sicking of armed guards on factory workers began to disappear. The anti-union shock troops of the Pinkertons turned to private eye work and Pearl Bergoff and his goons went out of business.

As John L. Lewis surveyed the scene when the 1930s drew to a close, he could mark off the worst hurdles as crossed. Despite the stubborn resistance that still lingered in Little Steel, despite confrontations elsewhere in industry, labor in the main had won its quest for recognition. The cost had been heavy; it had entailed the calling of 22,658 strikes in that single decade, the loss of scores of lives and the infliction of uncounted injuries. But by the end of 1937, unions had recruited 7.7 million workers who won contracts guaranteeing wages, hours and safety measures in every kind of company. To the millions of American workers who were mute and hog-tied at the outset of the decade, John L. Lewis' eloquent voice had given the power of speech. At one point Lewis even went so far as to administer a landmark scolding over nationwide radio to the President of the United States. During the Little Steel strike a reporter asked President Roosevelt for his views on the stalemate. "A plague o' both your houses," cried F.D.R. in exasperation, echoing the Shakespearean invocations of labor's champion.

John L. Lewis was not amused. "It ill behooves one who has supped at labor's table and who has been sheltered in labor's house," he roared over a network broadcast, "to curse with equal fervor and fine impartiality both labor and its adversaries when they become locked in deadly embrace."

Franklin D. Roosevelt heard Lewis loud and clear, and so did the rest of the nation. For by the end of this bloody decade American workers, once scattered and beaten by the industrial goons, ignored or opposed by politicians, had assumed their rightful places as first-class citizens.

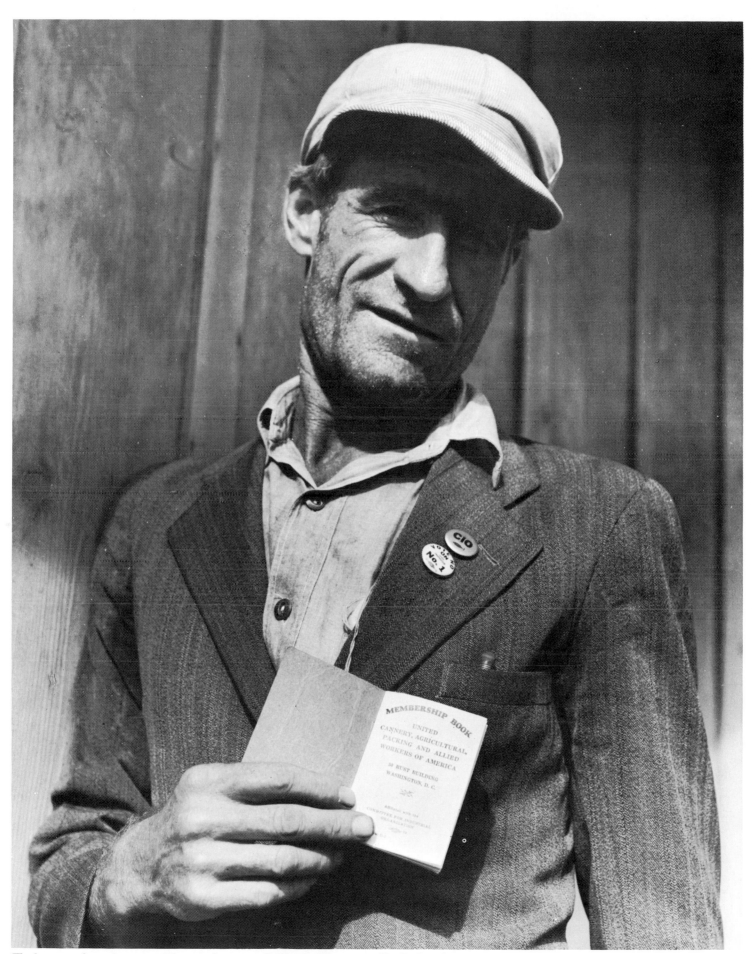

The long war for union recognition nearly over, a California laborer proudly displays his union membership book after a strike in November 1938.

The Movies

After a Saturday matinee, kids hug their door prizes.

Paradise in Celluloid

The American film has served as propaganda for the emotional monotony, the naive morality, the sham luxury, the haphazard etiquette and the grotesque exaggeration of the comic, the sentimental and the acrobatic that are so common in the United States.

POET AND CRITIC JOHN GOULD FLETCHER

No one who spent his time at the movies during the '30s would ever have known that the nation was down in the dumps. In a typical Hollywood movie of the era, Bette Davis gave up "everything" for the man she loved and moved into a remodeled Vermont farmhouse that one sarcastic critic estimated would cost $12,000 a year just to operate. In other films the vestiges of the real, cruel world of the Depression were replaced by delightful fictions like Walt Disney's 1937 *Snow White and the Seven Dwarfs,* by lurid epics like Cecil B. DeMille's *Sign of the Cross* and *Cleopatra,* and by superspectacular musicals such as the 1933 *Flying Down to Rio,* in which a whole chorus of show girls in gauze uniforms danced on the wings of airplanes in flight.

Hollywood's brand of heaven on earth was a deliberate and enormously successful effort to provide escape. Some 85 million people a week seized on it, commonly paying 25 cents for a ticket (10 cents for kids). Local theaters enhanced the appeal of a night at the movies by offering double and even triple features and by giving away door prizes that ranged from coupons for free hairdos to shiny new automobiles. The religion of escape had its icons; Shirley Temple dolls *(pages 96, 97)* and rubber statuettes

of Disney's dwarfs sold in the millions. The high priestess of Hollywood was gossip Louella Parsons, who divulged her "exclusives" every week on her radio show. Every year thousands of pilgrims journeyed to Hollywood to make reverent tours of the homes of the stars.

Not only were American films devoutly escapist, they were also, after 1934, very clean. In that year America's Roman Catholic bishops banded together to form the National League of Decency and Hollywood cooperated with it by enforcing a long list of taboos. Long kisses, adultery, double beds, words like "damn" and "hell" and even nude babies were banned from films. Criminals could no longer triumph over decent citizens. A hoyden like Mae West could no longer croon "I Like a Man Who Takes His Time." The day of "family movies" was ushered in, featuring adorable youngsters like Shirley Temple, Mickey Rooney and Jane Withers. Jeanette MacDonald and Nelson Eddy—whom Hollywood cynics dubbed "The Iron Butterfly" and "The Singing Capon"—began to turn out a whole series of fluffy white operettas. Even the titles of motion pictures were cleaned up; thus *Good Girls Go to Paris Too* became *Good Girls Go to Paris* and *Infidelity,* by a miraculous transformation, turned into *Fidelity.*

1932	1933	1934	1935	1936	1937	1938	1939	1940
MARIE DRESSLER	MARIE DRESSLER	WILL ROGERS	SHIRLEY TEMPLE	SHIRLEY TEMPLE	SHIRLEY TEMPLE	SHIRLEY TEMPLE	MICKEY ROONEY	MICKEY ROONEY
JANET GAYNOR	WILL ROGERS	CLARK GABLE	WILL ROGERS	CLARK GABLE	CLARK GABLE	CLARK GABLE	TYRONE POWER	SPENCER TRACY
JOAN CRAWFORD	JANET GAYNOR	JANET GAYNOR	CLARK GABLE	ASTAIRE-ROGERS	ROBERT TAYLOR	SONJA HENIE	SPENCER TRACY	CLARK GABLE
CHARLES FARRELL	EDDIE CANTOR	WALLACE BEERY	ASTAIRE-ROGERS	ROBERT TAYLOR	BING CROSBY	MICKEY ROONEY	CLARK GABLE	GENE AUTRY
GRETA GARBO	WALLACE BEERY	MAE WEST	JOAN CRAWFORD	JOE E. BROWN	WILLIAM POWELL	SPENCER TRACY	SHIRLEY TEMPLE	TYRONE POWER
NORMA SHEARER	JEAN HARLOW	JOAN CRAWFORD	CLAUDETTE COLBERT	DICK POWELL	JANE WITHERS	ROBERT TAYLOR	BETTE DAVIS	JAMES CAGNEY
WALLACE BEERY	CLARK GABLE	BING CROSBY	DICK POWELL	JOAN CRAWFORD	ASTAIRE-ROGERS	MYRNA LOY	ALICE FAYE	BING CROSBY
CLARK GABLE	MAE WEST	SHIRLEY TEMPLE	WALLACE BEERY	CLAUDETTE COLBERT	SONJA HENIE	JANE WITHERS	ERROL FLYNN	WALLACE BEERY
WILL ROGERS	NORMA SHEARER	MARIE DRESSLER	JOE E. BROWN	JEANETTE MACDONALD	GARY COOPER	ALICE FAYE	JAMES CAGNEY	BETTE DAVIS
JOE E. BROWN	JOAN CRAWFORD	NORMA SHEARER	JAMES CAGNEY	GARY COOPER	MYRNA LOY	TYRONE POWER	SONJA HENIE	JUDY GARLAND

Year-by-year charts of top 10 box-office stars, begun in 1932 by "Motion Picture Herald," show Gable's durability, Shirley Temple's rise and fall.

181

Slinky Jean Harlow gazes longingly at herself in "Dinner at Eight." Called the "Blonde Bombshell," she was the sexiest siren of the early '30s.

Sexiest male, by popular acclaim, was Clark Gable, shown here in his costume for the part of Mr. Christian in "Mutiny on the Bounty."

Some connoisseurs of Hollywood beauty preferred the shapely legs of Marlene Dietrich—shown here in "Blonde Venus"—to Harlow's slithery appeal.

Gary Cooper, all done up for his role in the 1935 thriller "Lives of a Bengal Lancer," rivaled Gable at the box-office as Hollywood's top he-man.

JEZEBEL

MARKED WOMAN

PETRIFIED FOREST

The Versatile Vixen

Very likely the most talented star of the decade was a popeyed little dynamo named Bette Davis. Though her own personality was so strong that every screen character she played, from *The Old Maid* to *Jezebel*, was unmistakably Bette Davis, she was nevertheless able to inject a biting realism into a remarkable range of roles. Off-screen she was every bit as strong-willed and sharp-tongued as the characters she played in her films. Her leading man Errol Flynn once commented to her, "I'd love to proposition you, Bette, but I'm afraid you'd laugh at me." Bette responded sweetly, "You're so right, Errol."

OF HUMAN BONDAGE

DARK VICTORY

JUAREZ

THE OLD MAID

186

Errol Flynn leers at the Virgin Queen in "The Private Lives of Elizabeth and Essex," in which Bette Davis played the 60-year-old monarch.

Sing a Song of Money

In the celluloid paradise created by Hollywood, some of the purest bits of froth were the musicals. These came in several delicious flavors, one fan favorite being the supercolossal productions of Busby Berkeley, which usually were built around love-birds Dick Powell and Ruby Keeler *(page 190)*. Another sticky-sweet variety featured Jeanette MacDonald and Nelson Eddy in schmaltzy operettas.

The biggest money-makers, however, were Fred Astaire and Ginger Rogers. Before they were teamed up, Ginger had played only a few feature parts. The report on Fred's first Hollywood screen test had read: "Can't act. Slightly bald. Can dance a little." But the first film in which they starred, *The Gay Divorcée* in 1934, turned out to be such a smash that RKO insured Fred's legs for a million dollars. By the end of the decade, the team had tapped its way through seven more hits; Astaire was branching out to start a chain of dance studios and Ginger was striking out on her own as an award-winning dramatic actress.

Nelson Eddy sings a duet with Jeanette MacDonald in "Rose Marie."

188

In the 1938 film "Carefree," Fred Astaire and Ginger Rogers perform a step called the Yam, which one magazine suggested fans learn for home parties.

Dick Powell and his fellow West Point cadets serenade Ruby Keeler and a flock of other innocents in the 1934 musical "Flirtation Walk."

Setting off an orgy of patriotism, Eleanor Powell sings Cole Porter's "Swingin' the Jinx Away," in the 1936 musical "Born to Dance."

Fiddling fairies swirl in "Gold Diggers of 1933." This sequence is typical of the choreography of Busby Berkeley, master of '30s musicals.

The Lovables

In the late '30s a frantic, fumbling, but good-natured tow-head name Andy Hardy was everybody's favorite teenager. Ably portrayed by Mickey Rooney, Andy was a romanticized image of the typical American boy; small wonder that though he hailed from the mythical town of Carvel, millions of fans felt that he really lived just down the block. His first movie, *A Family Affair*, convinced MGM that it had a hit; the studio quickly spun out a series of Andy Hardy films that helped make Mickey Rooney the industry's No. 1 box-office attraction in 1939 and 1940.

Always alert to new bonanzas, Hollywood immediately began producing such other groups of films as the hospital tear-jerker *Dr. Kildare*, the comic-strip inspired *Blondie* and the tenement-based *Dead End Kids*. Besides their box-office benefits, these series provided steady work for the squadrons of players the studios had under contract; thus the Hardy series kept busy not only Rooney but also Lewis Stone as paterfamilias Judge Hardy, Fay Holden as Mother Hardy and Cecilia Parker as sister Marian. Because of the simplicity of the roles, the series also were perfect places to allow new talent to gain experience; for example, the 1938 *Love Finds Andy Hardy (below)* showcased ingénues Judy Garland as Betsy, Lana Turner as siren Cynthia and Ann Rutherford as Andy's girl Polly.

1. *Would you buy a used car from this man? Andy Hardy, needing some wheels for a big dance, does.*

2. *Andy's flame, Polly, is so pleased with his buy she accepts the dance date and lets him kiss her.*

3. *In one bad evening, Andy learns his grandmother is ill and Polly breaks the date to go out of town.*

4. *Vacation-bound pal Beezy, afraid that his girl Cynthia will stray, hires Andy to "date her up."*

5. *Smitten by affable Cynthia, Andy forgets Polly and persuades Beezy's girl to go to the big dance.*

6. *As a favor, Andy dates a neighbor's visiting granddaughter, Betsy, whom he thinks "a mere child."*

7. *On a date, Andy swims while Cynthia watches; the lady also eschews tennis and roller skating.*

8. *Cynthia's one sport is smooching—soon, Andy frets that too much kissing will harm his health.*

9. *Meanwhile, car payments are stacking up, and Andy unburdens himself to a stern Judge Hardy.*

10. *The family hears from Mrs. Hardy, who is with her sick mother, that Andy's grandmother is worse.*

11. *Later, they learn by ham radio—Mrs. Hardy is far from a phone—that grandmother is much better.*

12. *Meanwhile, Beezy writes he is through with Cynthia. Betsy, falling for Andy, plots to move in.*

13. *Wily Betsy gets Cynthia to break her date and Polly returns to scold Andy for his brief infidelity.*

14. *Dateless, Andy asks Betsy, who sings so well at the dance she—and Andy—lead the Grand March.*

15. *Happy ending: Betsy goes home, contrite Polly returns to Andy and Judge Hardy finances the car.*

Armed with various gifts, Paul Muni (left) as "Scarface" and a henchman, played by George Raft, prepare to pay a farewell call on a hospitalized rival.

Crime Pays

The 1930 crime film *Little Caesar* taught movie producers that multiple murders meant multiple box-office dollars. *Caesar* set off a spate of gangster films whose swaggering stars were accused of schooling a generation of real-life punks. Hollywood, to duck accusations it was glorifying the underworld, always knocked off the crime lord in the last reel. But censors were unmoved and films glorifying gangsters died of official disapproval and public boredom.

Machine-gun bullets slam into Edward G. Robinson as "Little Caesar."

"Public Enemy" James Cagney persuades a bar owner to buy his booze.

Mae West tries her best to look coy as W.C. Fields offers a few sly suggestions in "My Little Chickadee," a Western spoof larded with Fieldisms.

The Funnymen

My Little Chickadee

*During the '30s Hollywood developed
the full spectrum of film comedy. The best was the slapstick
of the Marx Brothers (overleaf) and the low-key
love satires like those excerpted here. In a memorable scene from
"My Little Chickadee," snake-oil peddler
Cuthbert J. Twillie (W.C. Fields) chances upon a social
outcast named Flower Belle Lee (Mae West).*

Fields: Nice day.

West: Is it?

Fields: Course it's only one man's opinion. May I present my card?

West: Novelties and notions. What kind of notions you got?

Fields: You'd be surprised. Some are old, some are new. Whom have I the honor of addressing, my lady?

West: Mmmm—they call me Flower Belle.

Fields: Flower Belle. What a euphonious appellation—easy on the ears and a banquet for the eyes.

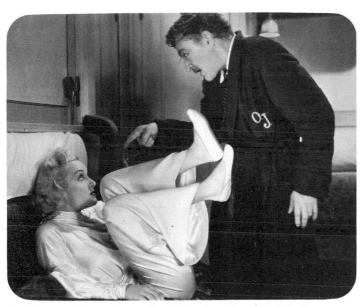

Curling up in her pajamas, Carole Lombard fends off John Barrymore.

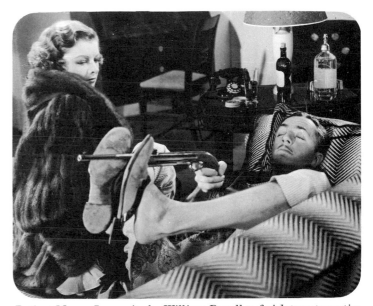

Patient Myrna Loy waits for William Powell to finish target practice.

Twentieth Century

*On the famous train, Broadway impresario Barrymore
meets Carole Lombard, an ex-love he had
made a star. He tries to woo her back by outlining a
wild religious play in which she will star.*

*Barrymore: I'm going to have Judas strangle himself with a
hair. I want to stagger New York with 100 camels and real sand
—brought from the Holy Land—and we'll have a Babylonian
banquet where you're covered with emeralds from head to foot
and nothing else. You go directly into your snake dance—it's perfect, but it's nothing compared to the finish, where you stand in
rags and the Emperor Nero himself offers you half his empire.
The last we see of you is as a pathetic little figure selling olives
on the—*
Lombard: You're craaazzzzy!

The Thin Man

*Having been tagged as a suspect in a murder,
detective Nick Charles (William Powell) swaps bons mots
as he toys with the gun he has received as a
Christmas present from his wife Nora (Myrna Loy).*

Loy: I'm glad you're not on this case.
Powell: The point is, I'm in it. They think I did it.
Loy: Well, didn't you?
(Powell shoots out half a dozen Christmas tree ornaments.)
*Loy: You're not in a shooting gallery. (Picking up a newspaper)
Finished with this?*
*Powell: Yes, and I know as much about the murder as they do.
So I'm a hero; I was shot twice in the "Tribune."*
Loy: And I read you were shot five times in the tabloid.
Powell: It's not true. He didn't come near my tabloid.

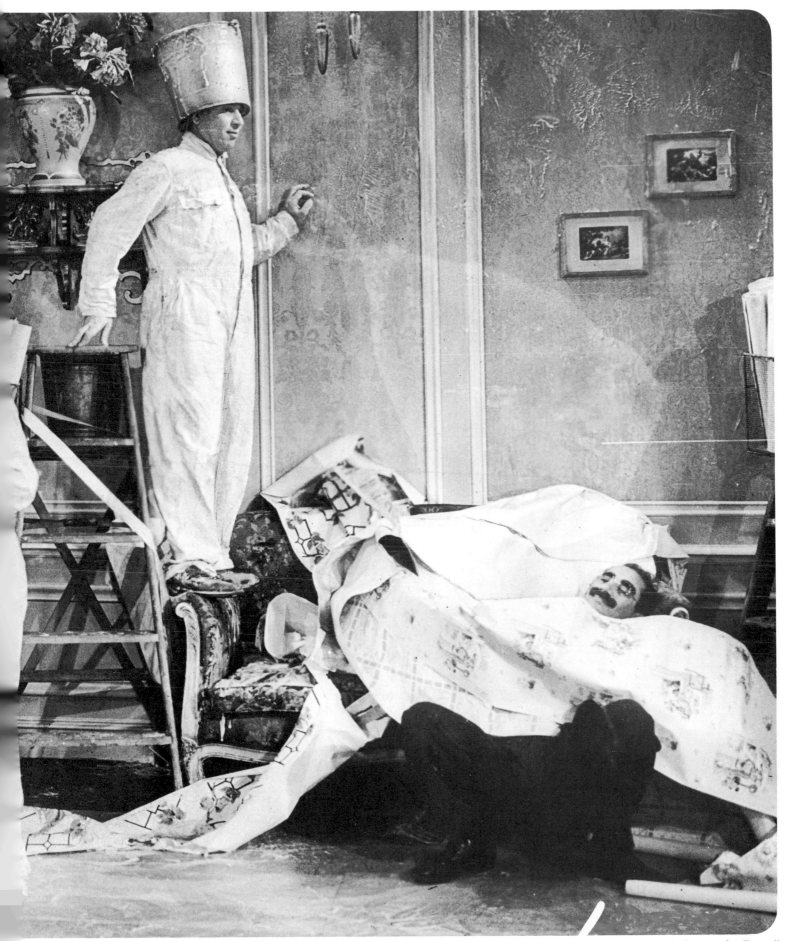

Esther Muir cringes amid the chaos produced by the Marx Brothers—Groucho (right), Harpo (center) and Chico—in "A Day at the Races."

Snow White inspects the dwarfs' hands before dinner. The leader of the dwarfs was Doc (far left); the audience favorite was Dopey (far right).

Animated Fantasy

Hollywood's retreat from reality climaxed in Walt Disney's first feature-length cartoon, *Snow White and the Seven Dwarfs*. Disney and his legion of animators started work on the movie in 1934, and for a long time it seemed they might never make it. Financiers were reluctant to lend them the nearly two million dollars they needed. Friends and enemies warned Disney that the public would never pay to sit through an 80-minute fairy tale.

But when the movie was finally unreeled after three years in production, kids of all ages flocked to watch the amiable cavorting of Disney's dwarfs and to swoon over Prince Charming. The movie quickly broke all previous attendance records, grossed eight million dollars and was translated into 10 languages. Critics, too, were ecstatic, not only about the brilliant animation, but also about the musical score (including "Heigh Ho," "Whistle While You Work," and "Some Day My Prince Will Come"). So vivid were some of the sequences that Radio City Music Hall, according to one legend, had to reupholster all seats after the movie's run; apparently so many children were terrified by Snow White's wicked stepmother that the seats were thoroughly drenched after each performance.

Prince Charming revives Snow White after her stepmother poisons her.

The Movies

Jimmy Stewart, the star of "Mr. Smith Goes to Washington," accuses Claude Rains of corruption.

Great Moments

Everyone who went to the movies left with memories of favorite scenes. Here are a few of the most vivid.

John Wayne leaps for the reins of the "Stagecoach" team after marauding Indians have shot the driver.

Halliwell Hobbs, in toga, and painter Spring Byington play zanies in "You Can't Take It with You."

In "Nothing Sacred," Fredric March socks Carole Lombard, first glamor girl to be hit in the movies.

"Algiers" fugitive Charles Boyer implores girlfriend Hedy Lamarr to run away with him from the Casbah.

An impromptu room divider keeps Clark Gable from Claudette Colbert in "It Happened One Night."

Shirley Temple, star of "Rebecca of Sunnybrook Farm," tap dances with Bill (Bojangles) Robinson.

Atop the Empire State Building "King Kong" swats at attacking planes just before they shoot him down.

Garbo talks: as "Anna Christie," Greta speaks for the first time in the movies: "Gif me a viskey, . . ."

Pouty Jean Harlow is told to shape up or else by angry husband Wallace Beery in "Dinner at Eight."

Charlie Chaplin defiantly gags it up as an enormous machine nearly devours him in "Modern Times."

Lead-slinging Tyrone Power, as "Jesse James," leads his outlaws in a getaway from a bank heist.

As a fisherman in "Captains Courageous," Spencer Tracy croons to castaway Freddy Bartholomew.

Charles Laughton snarls at Clark Gable when trouble starts to simmer in "Mutiny on the Bounty."

Off to see "The Wizard of Oz," Judy Garland chats with Bert Lahr; Jack Haley and Ray Bolger listen.

On the lam, Humphrey Bogart and two armed sidekicks terrorize a roadhouse in "The Petrified Forest."

Gloria Stewart meets "The Invisible Man" (Claude Rains), whose face appears only at the movie's end.

The "Union Pacific" meets the Central Pacific and the first transcontinental rail route is completed.

Bon vivant Melvyn Douglas is so charming that he makes even the dour Garbo laugh in "Ninotchka."

"The Plainsman," Gary Cooper, submits to Indian torture rather than divulge the cavalry's location.

Director Alfred Hitchcock plays a cameo in his film "Rebecca" by eavesdropping on George Sanders.

In a fiery speech, Paul Muni defends the French martyr Alfred Dreyfus in "The Life of Émile Zola."

Bela Lugosi as "Dracula," the Transylvanian vampire, closes in on a particularly tempting throat.

As "Captain Blood," swashbuckling Errol Flynn parries Basil Rathbone's attempt to run him through.

Rosalind Russell yanks Paulette Goddard's hair to start a wild female fight scene in "The Women."

British nurse Helen Hayes is smitten by Gary Cooper, the wounded officer of "A Farewell to Arms."

No beauty herself, Elsa Lanchester recoils at the thought of becoming "The Bride of Frankenstein."

Marlene Dietrich, flashing a famous gam, tries to kick Jimmy Stewart in "Destry Rides Again."

"Public Enemy" James Cagney stops the early-morning nagging of Mae Clarke with a grapefruit.

Margaret Mitchell, the author of "Gone with the Wind," meets Clark Gable, the actor who played her swashbuckling character, Rhett Butler.

Marching through Georgia

OLIVIA DE HAVILLAND AS MELANIE

THOMAS MITCHELL AS MR. O'HARA

SEARCHLIGHTS PLAY ON ATLANTA'S GRAND THEATER ON OPENING NIGHT.

LESLIE HOWARD AS ASHLEY

HATTIE McDANIEL AS MAMMY

The most expensive and most discussed movie of the '30s was *Gone with the Wind*. The picture had its première on December 15, 1939, in Atlanta, Georgia, the city where much of the film's Civil War action was set. For years people had been awaiting the opening night. Producer David O. Selznick had bought the screen rights to Margaret Mitchell's novel in 1936 and then ballyhooed his project by conducting a nationwide hunt for a new face to play the heroine, Scarlett O'Hara. About 1,400 girls were interviewed and the public wrote in thousands of suggestions. When Vivien Leigh was finally chosen, screams of outrage arose because she was English and not American.

Then came the world première. The theater had been rebuilt to resemble a mansion featured in the film, and pretty usherettes wore hoop skirts. And when Miss Leigh appeared on the screen, the old outrage turned to adoration. The feeling quickly spread to the other stars *(above)* and to the show itself. After the show was over, the president-general of the United Daughters of the Confederacy announced: "No one can quarrel now with the selection of Miss Leigh as Scarlett. She is Margaret Mitchell's Scarlett to the life. The whole thing has me overcome."

Vivien Leigh, as Scarlett O'Hara, runs across the lawn of her plantation, Tara, after she learns the man she loves is marrying another girl.

A comrade reads the "Sunday Worker" in Communist headquarters in New York.

The Panacea Seekers

The Nazi salute is the coming salute for the whole United States.
FRITZ KUHN, PRESIDENT OF THE GERMAN-AMERICAN BUND, 1938

With capitalism apparently collapsed around its feet, with its traditional leaders and formulas wiped out, a sizable segment of the country was frantically seeking new ways of doing things. The quest was reflected in the letters full of plans for beating the Depression that poured onto F.D.R.'s desk. A surprising majority of them shared a basic premise: that the United States had a marvelous productive system just aching to create abundance for all. What had to be changed were the financial and political institutions that somehow clogged this horn of plenty.

Thus the search for a remedy to the country's problem started as a kind of innocent democratic exercise, involving a variety of odd people and odd ideas. In Greenwich Village there was leather-coated engineer Howard Scott proposing, in 1932, a social scheme he called Technocracy, that would increase the wealth tenfold by substituting energy units called ergs and joules for dollars and cents. In Royal Oak, Michigan, there was the Reverend Charles E. Coughlin plumping for an inflationary, silver-backed currency; from the Louisiana bayous Huey Long *(overleaf)* was planning to ride into the White House on his "Share Our Wealth" nostrum. In Hollywood and New York there were the earnest intellectuals lapping up, with various de-

grees of innocence, an even more powerful share-the-wealth concept at Communist-run meetings. In California there was Dr. Francis Townsend, an old frontier doctor who would take care of old people—not to mention the whole economy—by giving each citizen over 60 the sum of $200 monthly to be spent within 30 days.

As the decade wore on, however, the innocence began to fade and some of the Messiahs began to appear in very different guises. Coughlin, for one, gradually slid so far to the political right that his lectures dealt less with economics than with Jew-baiting. Many others decided that Adolf Hitler was the real Messiah; and they closed ranks with the Berlin-directed German-American Bund, aping the Nazis' salutes *(right)*, the colored shirts and the broad-gauge racism. As for the Communists, their Soviet idols made a 1939 alliance with Hitler—an ideological turn-about that caused massive disillusionment with people's democracy. By decade's end the seeking after panaceas was about over, for it had become clear that there really weren't any. Furthermore, with the economy alive and progressing, the need seemed no longer urgent, and Americans returned to the practice of leaving politics in the traditional hands of Democratic and Republican politicians.

A German-American Bundist salutes a New Jersey audience at a 1938 Washington's Birthday rally. Bundists called Washington "the first Fascist."

Huey Long, the cocky governor of Louisiana, had few peers as a campaigner. A tireless hand-shaker, he also twisted arms when the need arose.

The Pied Piper of the Bayous

Almost everybody outside of Louisiana saw its governor, Huey Long, as the outrageous demagogue and dictator he was. An unabashed egotist who called himself the Kingfish after a pompous radio character of the day, he ran the state with a capricious will backed by the guns of the police. However, to the poor farmers who made up the state's largest bloc of voters, Long was an infallible friend.

Long's mass appeal was based on a dreamy program, to which he gave the alluring name "Share Our Wealth." Theoretically, Huey would take from the rich and give to the poor. In actual practice, he levied many consumer taxes that, as always, hit the poor the hardest; and he increased the state deficit by almost $100 million.

Long also sold himself a dream—that he would become the President of the Yew-nited States. Huey felt so certain of it that he wrote a wool-gathering book entitled *My First Days in the White House*. This arrogant fantasy appears in excerpt below. Unhappily for the Kingfish, his dream would not come true, for he was shot dead by a constituent who could endure no more of Long's predations.

Soon after I had sent the cabinet names to the Senate, my secretary informed me that Mr. Hoover was trying to get me on the telephone. . . . I heard the voice of that Quaker gentleman say: "Er-r-r, Mr. President—er-r-r, this is Hoover. Is it true that you have tendered me the position of Secretary of Commerce?"

I said I had sent his name to the Senate.

"But, Mr. President, I should have been consulted. This has placed me in a very embarrassing position."

"In what way, Mr. Hoover?" I inquired.

"Why, I am a former President of the United States, and it's a terrible step down for me to be asked to serve in your cabinet," he replied.

"Just what is your position in public life today, Mr. Hoover?"

He hesitated and then: "Well, suppose I decline on the ground that I do not care to be associated with you?"

"All right, Mr. Hoover," I replied. "That is something for you to decide in your own conscience."

Mr. Hoover's voice lost its angry tone. "All right, Mr. President," he replied. "I will consider it."

Some minutes after ten o'clock that night I was called to the telephone. I heard a voice: "Hello, Kingfish!"

It was Franklin D. Roosevelt. "Yes, Mr. President," I answered.

"What in the world do you mean by offering me a cabinet post, after all the things you have said about me as President?"

"I only offered you a position which I thought you were qualified to fill."

"Well, it's a terrible fall from the Presidency to the Secretaryship of the Navy," he replied.

"You sound just like Hoover," I said, "but he couldn't call to mind any position he held just now."

"Well, Huey, I'll have to give this more consideration," the former President told me. "I had a statement all prepared here, declining, but I'll destroy it. Say, suppose I accept and fail to become the best Secretary? What's the penalty then?"

"In that case," I replied, "people will hold me responsible, and they may punish me for your failure."

The former President chuckled: "Well, Huey, that's almost reason enough to accept the position. You'll hear from me later."

My worries about the completion of my cabinet being almost over, I undertook to set in motion my plan for a redistribution of the nation's wealth.

HUEY LONG, *MY FIRST DAYS IN THE WHITE HOUSE*, 1935

Radio's Political Priest

As a political speaker, Father Charles E. Coughlin was second in popularity only to President Roosevelt. Millions listened to the priest's angry tirades and radical schemes for sharing the wealth, broadcast every Sunday from the Shrine of the Little Flower at Royal Oak, Michigan. In 1934, when Coughlin launched his own party, the National Union for Social Justice, more than five million listeners signed up within two months.

Though Coughlin was "for" social justice, among other causes, he was better known by the things he was against.

First and last, he was anti-Communist. He became violently anti-Roosevelt, calling the President a "great betrayer" because the New Deal allegedly had "communistic tendencies." Coughlin made anti-Semitic remarks about "the Jewish bankers," and he also attacked both the labor unions and the industrial capitalists.

These views were met by a rising storm of protest. Under pressure from all quarters, Coughlin slowly curtailed his political activities; and by mid-1940 the air ceased to crackle with fulminations like the excerpts below.

President Roosevelt has both compromised with the money changers and conciliated with monopolistic industry. This spirit of compromise has been the predominant weakness of our present leadership to such an extent that it has not disdained to hold out the olive branch to those whose policies are crimsoned with the theories of sovietism and international socialism.

We cannot applaud a New Deal which, with all its chaotic implications, submits either to the supremacy of a financial overlord more obnoxious than King George III or to the red slavery of an economic Simon Legree.　　　　　MARCH 1935

As far as the National Union is concerned, no candidate which is endorsed for Congress can campaign, go electioneering for, or support the great betrayer and liar, Franklin D. Roosevelt, he who promised to drive the money changers from the temple and succeeded in driving the farmers from their homesteads and the citizens from their homes in the cities.

He who promised to drive the money changers from the temple has built up the greatest debt in history, $35,000,000,000, which he permitted the bankers the right, without restriction, to spend, and for which he contracted that you and your children shall repay with seventy billion hours of labor.

I ask you to purge the man who claims to be a Democrat from the Democratic party, and I mean Franklin Double-Crossing Roosevelt.　　　　　JULY 1936

When any upstart dictator in the U.S. succeeds in making this a one party form of government, when the ballot is useless, I shall have the courage to stand up and advocate the use of bullets. Mr. Roosevelt is a radical. The Bible commands "increase and multiply," but Mr. Roosevelt says to destroy and devastate. Therefore I call him anti-God.　　　　　SEPTEMBER 1936

If we are sincere, we will recall all the Ambassadors and Ministers from the communist countries, from Mexico, from Barcelona, in whose suburbs 300 innocent nuns—the breath of life still in their bodies—were drenched with kerosene and burned.

I say to the good Jews of America, be not indulgent with the irreligious, atheistic Jews and Gentiles who promote the cause of persecution in the land of the Communists, the same ones who promote the cause of atheism in America. Yes, be not lenient with your high financiers and politicians who assisted at the birth of the only . . . system in all civilization that adopted atheism as its religion . . . and slavery as its liberty.　　　　　NOVEMBER 1938

Father Charles E. Coughlin carries the political battle to his many enemies. Later he admitted, "It was a horrible mistake to enter politics."

Communist leader "Mother" Bloor, shown with beauty contest winners, was prized by Reds for her deep-dish American look and colonial forebears.

The Very Red-blooded Americans

In the spring of 1937 the New York chapter of the D.A.R. unaccountably failed to celebrate the 162nd anniversary of Paul Revere's ride. On the appointed day, however, hooves clattered along Broadway and into view cantered a horse with a rider attired in Continental costume. He carried a sign: "The DAR forgets but the YCL remembers." The YCL stood for the Young Communist League and the incident stood for the zany fact that during the four years between 1935 and 1939, nobody worked harder at being American than the American Communists. They frenetically tried to build an image of the Party as a native American organization, made up of just plain folks who were anxious to cooperate with other patriots. Explained a YCL leaflet at the University of Wisconsin: "Some people have the idea that a YCLer is politically minded, that nothing outside of politics means anything. Gosh no. We go to shows, parties and all that. The YCL and its members are no different from other people."

The sudden transformation of the local Bolsheviki into 200 per cent Americans began in 1935 in, of all places, Moscow, and for all its absurd contradictions was a serious matter. Realizing that Hitler meant one day to attack Russia, the Soviets shelved their traditional anti-capitalist dogma and ordered Communists the world over to form the widest possible alliances to protect the Red motherland. The new line was called the Popular Front and the U.S. Party skillfully carried it out. Whisking out of sight its bias against capitalism and the American social system, the Party donned a cheerful, homespun exterior and began waving the U.S. flag. Communists trotted out such respectable symbols as Ella Reeves (Mother) Bloor, daughter of a Republican banker, to give themselves a flavor of old-established Americanism and to help woo others with WASP names and Mayflower lineages. New York units joined black churches in organizing Mother's Day observances, and the *Daily Worker* inaugurated a super-American sports section.

Different organizations called "fronts" were set up to attract ordinary Americans of every persuasion. Fronts were established to further the interests of medical interns, folksingers, theater buffs, book club joiners and so on. At their peak, the fronts had more than seven million members, represented over 1,000 affiliated organizations, and had acquired a certain respectability. The 1939 congress of the American League against War and Fascism was welcomed in Washington both by the Secretary of the Interior and the Grand Exalted Ruler of the Elks.

Hollywood was where the Popular Front really kicked up dust. After studio hours the chic neighborhoods of Beverly Hills buzzed with activities for a variety of causes, some of enduring value: the Hollywood Anti-Nazi League, the Screen Writers' Guild, the Theatre Committee for the Defense of the Spanish Republic. Stars, many of them unaware of being Red dupes, threw open their hearts, homes and swimming pools so that Hollywood's Popular Front offered an irresistible bargain—an opportunity to combine social climbing with do-gooding. Where else could lowly and lonely liberals rub bosoms and shoulders with the likes of Myrna Loy, Joan Crawford, Franchot Tone, Edward G. Robinson, James Cagney and Melvyn Douglas? The film community welcomed the sensation of being involved with real history and gave generously of time and money. Benefits for the Abraham Lincoln Brigade, a group of Americans who volunteered to fight the Nazi-backed armies of General Francisco Franco in the Spanish Civil War, never yielded less than $5,000 to $8,000. And there was the memorable night when the editor of the Communist magazine *New Masses* appealed for funds at a bigwig's home and came away with $20,000.

It was great fun while it lasted. But on August 23, 1939, in another spectacular about-face, Russia signed with Germany the Nazi-Soviet pact and Stalin toasted Hitler's health: "I know how much the German nation owes to its Fuehrer." At that shocking piece of double-think, the ideological ground beneath the Popular Front gave way, and it soon collapsed. Within a few months the American Communist Party lost thousands of members, especially among the intellectuals; and many thousands of other Americans who had been pursuing good causes under a Red banner awoke to the realization that they'd been had.

The End of a Crusade

When the fascist General Franco, supported by both Hitler and Mussolini, marched to overthrow Spain's Republican Government, idealistic Americans sided strongly with the Republicans. More than 3,000 American men went to Spain to fight in a volunteer unit called the Abraham Lincoln Brigade. Below are excerpts from the letters home of one volunteer, Wilfred Mendelson of Brooklyn, who was killed in action July 28, 1938.

June 3, 1938

I am writing from the training base of the Spanish People's Army. Last night we marched into the nearby town. The older women, careworn faces, thinking of their own sons and husbands at the front, cried. The young girls smiled or raised arms in the popular salute. Our 4,000-mile journey was being understood, appreciated.

June 5, 1938

Sunday in Spain. It is very quiet, almost blissful.

June 22, 1938

About myself, I am doing fine, a good shot really, like a Coney Island range expert. This summer may well seal the fate of world peace. Everybody must be brought to the realization that every day Spain continues in its efforts time is gained for the peace forces all over. In this light Spain is holding the fort for America. If America does not rally it is cutting its own throat.

July 15, 1938

I've seen a magnificent cathedral rising through Barcelona completely stripped of interior and exterior. But that can convey nothing to me. My brain says "Bombers", I know it, I see it, but the terror just isn't there.

July 23, 1938

Looks like any hour now we'll be off. While our forces are tremendously strong and we confidently expect victory, accidents do happen to individuals. Don't show this note to my parents. Take care of them. I love you.

Veterans of the Abraham Lincoln Brigade, back home from Spain, give the Popular Front clenched-fist salute at a 1939 May Day parade.

E.H. Crump, the tough old pol who ran Memphis and dominated much of the rest of Tennessee, styled himself the champion of the "little" man.

Mister Ed Crump, He Runs This Town

When President Franklin D. Roosevelt carried his campaign for re-election into the South in September 1936, his entourage was joined by a big, genial man with a pink puckish face, flowing white hair and eyebrows as bushy as a guardsman's mustachios. This colorful creature was E.H. (Edward Hull) Crump, long-time boss of Memphis. At 61, Ed Crump was at the peak of his power, unbeatable in a fight or a frolic. In this last golden decade for big-city bosses, Crump ruled his bailiwick autocratically. Like his peers in Jersey City, Boston and a dozen other cities, he influenced decisions that affected the whole nation.

F.D.R. greeted the "Boss of Memphis" with the cordiality due one of the President's staunchest backers. But later, F.D.R. expressed concern over a recent bit of Crump pork-barreling, which had brought to Memphis a $15,000 municipal kennel paid for with federal funds.

"Well, Ed," said Roosevelt, "what about that dog house down in Memphis?"

Crump replied confidently, "It will mean a lot of votes for you down there."

The Boss was as good as his word. On election day, his private domain of Memphis and surrounding Shelby County contributed a whopping plurality of almost 60,000 votes to an easy Democratic victory in Tennessee. Only 2,194 voters failed to cast their ballots for Roosevelt.

Crump's delivery of the vote came as no surprise to Tennesseans. For three decades, the Boss and his political organization had been winning elections with monotonous regularity. Though Crump was retired, now, from elective position, he continued to run his machine from the offices of his large, prosperous insurance agency, E.H. Crump & Company; it functioned with such awesome efficiency that one reporter called it "a combined reaper, thresher and binder; a machine that has only one weakness—it's *too* perfect."

Such journalistic judgments irritated Crump but had little effect on his supporters. To most Memphians the Boss was courtly yet earthy, and they treated him with fondness or respect, rather like a fine old Southern landmark. As Crump often declared with a contented smile or a grand wave to passing constituents, "They like me."

But when Crump was at work in his company office, he left no doubt as to who ran the political show. In various meetings, phone calls and letters, he dispensed patronage, deployed his ward leaders, laid down policy guidelines for Crump men in state and national office. Benevolence was his stock-in-trade, ruthlessness his ace-in-the-hole. Any man who needed a loan or a job, and any firm seeking to do business with the city, would get a friendly hearing from the Boss, and they often got more.

Once Ed Crump had bestowed his favors, the recipients showed their appreciation by contributing to his next campaign or by buying insurance from E.H. Crump & Company. They heeded a rumor that Crump kept file cards to enforce voting orthodoxy. As one executive explained it, "He knows how everybody votes, and if a man doesn't

---

I probably have been successful in more elections than any other man in America. I was elected 25 times myself as police commissioner, mayor, congressman, county treasurer, etc., and have assisted in 92 other elections without a single defeat.

EDWARD HULL CRUMP

---

vote right, the machine can hit him through his kinfolks, because everybody has kinfolks at the public trough."

This general principle applied to high officials who owed their posts to Crump. They knew that anyone who departed from the Boss's basic tenets, such as his commitment to public ownership of the utilities, would be defeated in the next election by a more devout believer. Therefore Crump men were inclined to obey his every whim with gusto and alacrity. For example, Crump, a noted bird-lover, once exhorted Memphians to protect their feathered friends, and immediately his county commissioner rushed out to set traps for villainous tomcats.

Crump was, in all, the consummate machine politician. On this point almost everyone agreed, from the fiery minister who called him "the lowest down political boss inside or outside of hell," to the solid businessman who conceded, "He gives us good government." In fact the only notable demurrer was Crump himself. "Who said boss?" he once demanded of a tactless newsman. "I am just an unassuming good citizen working with and for the people."

Crump's angry response to bossism charges was at least understandable. The term "boss" had always implied extravagantly crooked dealings and dictatorial methods. And in the '30s, bosses were scaling new heights of venality and arrogance. Crump had good reason to resent being bracketed with the Vare brothers of Philadelphia

---

If you drive hard, others will hit the same stride. If you hesitate in forcing an organization, those down the line will also hesitate. Don't sit down in the meadow and wait for the cow to back up and be milked—Go after the cow.

CRUMP ON POLITICAL HUSBANDRY

---

or Bill Thompson of Chicago. They were extremely venal men and they were not the worst of the bosses.

In Jersey City, there was Mayor Frank Hague, who had ruled like a feudal baron since 1917. With no visible source of income but a salary of $8,500, he had become a millionaire several times over. Before each election he held a bald-faced shakedown; all municipal and county employees were dunned for contributions on peril of losing their jobs. According to investigators, up to 20 per cent of the Hague vote was cast in the name of people deceased or otherwise unqualified. For those who objected, Hague had a disdainful retort: "I am the law."

Kansas City had Thomas J. Pendergast. In order to afford horse bets of $10,000, Tom opened his town to vice lords and racketeers, from whom he could extort copious payoffs. However, the Internal Revenue bureau discovered that in a single year Tom had neglected to account for $443,550 as income. Sentenced as a tax evader in 1939, Pendergast languished in prison for 12 months; but the locals could not forget his standard promise to his detractors: "I'll break your jaw."

Boston was the stamping ground of James Michael Curley, a charming man who served often as mayor and twice

as a jailbird convicted of fraud. Curley's career was a whirl of patronage, litigation, scandal and gorgeous living. One year Jim was accused of spending $85,206 on cigars, dinners and traveling expenses. To him, and to many of his constituents, it was no crime that he paid for these simple necessities out of public funds.

Compared to such lurid grafters, Ed Crump was painfully honest and decorous. He doted on his wife and three sons; he never smoked and seldom drank anything stronger than Bulgarian buttermilk. In politics, the moral distinctions that he drew seemed esoteric to some, but he held to them. He always returned or paid for the gifts that came his way. He never profited personally by the contributions that lubricated his political machine, and he banished or prosecuted any Crump man who helped himself to the organization's regular collections from business houses, liquor stores and pinball operators. And yet Crump's long career was practically a blueprint for any strong man planning to assume undelegated authority.

Ed Crump was a rawboned farm boy of 19 when, in 1894, he left his home town of Holly Springs, Mississippi, for an office job in Memphis. He arrived with only 25 cents in his pocket. But his assets included a head for figures, consuming ambition and an enormous capacity for sustained labor. Within a decade Crump became owner of a carriage-making company, whose sale made him a budding capitalist. He also plunged into politics, ringing doorbells to get out the vote in Memphis' Fourth Ward. In the next few years he was elected councilman, then police commissioner, and won citywide approval for his aggressive campaigning. "Crump," wrote one reporter, "knows everybody and he shakes hands with everybody. He can cover more territory and be in more places at the same time than any man that entered the political game."

By 1909, Crump had emerged as a tough, smart politician, and, in the context of the times, a reformer. Memphis desperately needed some such man as mayor. The city groaned under a corrupt government; its tawdry streets were an open house for gamblers, sporting girls and violent thugs. Crump leaped into the mayoralty race on just the right platform: law and order, fiscal responsibility and new services for the hard-pressed "little people."

It was a rough, wild contest. Thugs charged Crump's meetings, and his boys had to fight them off in pitched battles. But Ed squeaked through by 79 votes, and loomed as the new power of mid-South politics.

In the course of time, Memphians learned that their new mayor was tough enough to keep his campaign promises. His revamped police force drove out the footpads, gamblers and fancy ladies. He broadened city thoroughfares, built schools and hospitals, parks and playgrounds. He accomplished all this partially through frugal contracting and partially by increasing the tax levies on "outside interests" such as utility companies, which had raked in their profits but had paid little more than token taxes.

Crump's whip-cracking leadership was bad news for loafers and other riffraff, and this fact was soon celebrated in two song classics. Down along the Mississippi, black dockhands chanted dolefully, "Mister Ed Crump, he runs this town." And on Beale Street in the black quarter, a jazz musician named W.C. Handy composed the lament known as "The Memphis Blues":

> *Mister Crump don't 'low no easy riders here,*
> *But we don't care what Mister Crump don't 'low,*
> *We gonna barrelhouse anyhow,*
> *'Cause Mister Crump don't 'low no easy riders here.*

Despite the severity of Crump's regime, his policies offered something appealing to almost everyone; and in six years as mayor and eight years as county commissioner he forged a powerful coalition of supporters. As was the case with many other bosses, the city's businessmen liked Crump because he insured the stability they needed for a thriving trade. The farmers not only liked him; they considered him their hero and protector—and a "ring-tailed tooter." And they, along with the low-paid industrial workers, cheered him to the echo whenever he joined a new battle in his righteous war against the "interests."

Crump gave them plenty to cheer about. His pals in Nashville pushed a state law fixing telephone rates, persuading the phone company to refund more than $100,000 to local clients. When a railroad failed to meet its contractual obligations, he marched out with a crowbar, tore up a section of track and set policemen to guard the road-

We teach people how to vote and urge them to vote. They don't know the candidates they want to vote for, and they don't know where to mark the ballot. If you put Judas Iscariot on the ballot, he'd get 1,000 votes in Shelby County.

CRUMP ON VOTER EDUCATION

block until the company capitulated. The locals loved it.

Of course the interests fought back. They hired the Pinkerton Detective Agency to burrow into Crump's dealings. But their best effort, a forced audit of the city's books, gave the Boss's backers yet another chance to cheer. The books were off only three cents—in Crump's favor.

Of all Crump's supporters, the most loyal were blacks, who constituted about 40 per cent of the population of Shelby County. It seemed to be an anomaly that blacks were voting en masse in Tennessee, while just across the line in Mississippi they were virtually disenfranchised by custom and the poll tax. Crump saw to it that the Memphis blacks voted, even if his organization had to pay their poll taxes. He gave them a hospital, named a park after the black abolitionist Frederick Douglass, and, above all, he fought the Ku Klux Klan.

Crump's actions were influenced by the fact that he relied heavily on black votes; but he was truly an egalitarian of sorts. He retained a Jewish lawyer, Will Gerber, as his trusted aide; and in 1928 he had angrily declared, "The man or woman who votes against Alfred E. Smith because he is a Catholic betrays his American citizenship and violates the letter and spirit of the Constitution." Somehow these attitudes caused little concern among Crump's redneck constituents. After all, the Boss was a dyed-in-the-cotton Southerner who could be counted on to maintain the important facets of the status quo.

In the '20s, Crump became strong enough to move toward statewide mastery. Blocking his way was Luke Lea,

225

the ruthless publisher of the Nashville *Tennessean,* and Crump took him on in a brisk backroom battle in the state capital. As one newspaper put it, "Mr. Crump came to Nashville on Sunday night as the boss of Shelby County. In two days' work, he was elected to the 'boss' of Tennessee politics." That was that.

Thus the opening years of the decade found Ed Crump riding the crest of hard-won success. For three years, he served as U.S. Congressman. But homesickness prompted the Boss to resign and return to his beloved Memphis. Here he fully enjoyed doing what came naturally—i.e., plain and fancy hometown politicking. He added new refinements to his powerful political machine, fought the interests, called for a better and prettier Memphis. Despising unnecessary noise in public places, he even banned horn tooting in traffic—and the city fell strangely silent.

As for those who risked Crump's wrath, they learned at their cost that he was a master of political invective. Indulging his fondness for purple abuse, the Boss said of three rivals, "This trio of mangy bubonic rats are conscienceless liars." Often he added a quotable insult to his famous output of rural wit. He impaled a renegade Crump man with the line, "That man would milk his neighbor's cow through a crack in the fence." When a pompous opponent campaigned on a creditable record made years back, Ed commented, "Even a buzzard is pure white until he is half grown."

Crump's enemies countered with exaggerated charges. They accused the Boss of neglecting to count many anti-Crump votes, of importing blacks from Arkansas to vote for his candidates. There was a tale that Crump and crony Will Gerber had been seen in a cemetery copying names off tombstones. According to the yarn, Gerber found one inscription illegible, but Crump insisted that he puzzle it out. "We've got to have the right name," said the Boss. "This has got to be an honest election."

In the '30s Crump won the victory that crowned his career. The cause was an old and dear one for him: cheap public power, publicly owned. In 1933 Congress had passed a New Deal measure setting up the Tennessee Valley Authority to provide rural electric power in the mid-South. At once Crump demanded—and Memphians soon endorsed overwhelmingly—a nine-million-dollar bond issue to pipe TVA power into the city.

But then the battle lines hardened. The private power lobby and its conservative allies did all they could to dilute and delay the effect of the TVA; Crump fought the spoilers at every turn and drove recalcitrant officeholders into action. When his current governor, Hill McAlister, was slow in appointing a committee to work with the TVA, Crump wrote him a firm letter, and McAlister nervously replied, "I suppose I had better do it right now."

Never put a sponge on the end of a hammer if you expect to drive a nail.   CRUMP ON POLITICAL PERSUASION

With a toss of his hoary head, Crump roared, "I propose to give TVA to all the homes, farms and factories and the Power Trust will not tell me how to do it."

By 1939, TVA was fairly safe. Crump—and the people of Tennessee—had finally won.

The victory came none too soon for old Ed Crump. Within a year, he was staggered by the deaths of his son John and his ancient mother. Afterward, his zest gradually waned, and his bitterness increased as various reporters, ignoring his positive contribution, constantly stigmatized him with the title "Boss." Except to the most loyal of his devoted constituents, he was no more than the best of a bad breed—or the worst product of America's glorious political tradition.

Either way, one thing was certain: before the '30s ended, Crump was a living anachronism. His style of leadership dated back a half-century and more, to a simpler time when politics was an intimate matter between friends, and when an elected official was often the neighbor or drinking companion in whom most people trusted. But by 1940, paternalism and cronyism were losing appeal; the voters, growing sophisticated, often crossed party lines to elect unbossed candidates of their own choosing. The great age of the bosses was drawing to a close.

A big spender, Boss Frank Hague of Jersey City gave himself a $125,000 home, his church a $50,000 altar, his town a $3,000,000 ball park.

Swing

Two swing musicians get top billing on a Broadway marquee.

The Big Bands Break Loose

It makes no diff'rence if it's sweet or hot, Just give that rhythm ev'rything you got.

Oh, it don't mean a thing, if it ain't got that swing.

"IT DON'T MEAN A THING" BY IRVING MILLS AND DUKE ELLINGTON

Before dawn one cold day in 1938, hundreds of teenagers started lining up in front of New York City's Paramount Theater, literally spilling out onto the street and stopping traffic. A special squad of cops was called to contain the "riot." The riot outside was nothing compared with the one that soon broke loose inside. When the early morning movie was over, a band on an elevating platform rose out of the orchestra pit; 3,000 adolescents screamed and, as the musicians opened up, began to dance in the aisles. The band was Benny Goodman's, and the music he was playing was "swing."

In the closing years of the decade, all of America was swept by swing fever. In little towns girls in loose skirts and saddle shoes tripped into ice-cream parlors with their boyfriends, plugged nickels into the jukebox and set the place rocking with their intricate jitterbug dance steps. Radio audiences clustered around their sets to hear their favorite bands *(pages 232-233)* on weekly programs, and on Saturdays they tuned in *Your Hit Parade* to learn the top 10 hits of the week. *The New York Times* solemnly suggested that the craze was getting out of hand, quoting a psychologist on the "dangerously hypnotic influence of swing, cunningly devised to a faster tempo than seventy-two bars to the minute—faster than the human pulse."

Actually, swing was nothing more than jazz under a new name. Black groups in the '20s had developed jazz, which was characterized by a driving rhythm and improvised solos; but few white people heard anything except tame orchestrated versions of it. During the Depression the authentic jazz sound went completely underground. The record industry almost died out. Many jazz musicians found jobs playing bland music in radio studios. Then, in 1934, Benny Goodman, who was only 24 years old, formed a band to play the real jazz to mass audiences. The band's first cross-country tour in 1935 was a string of disasters. By the time the group had reached California, it had returned to playing innocuous dance music. At the end of an evening at the Palomar Ballroom in Hollywood, however, Goodman was so disgusted with syrupy music that he told his sidemen to swing for one set to close the evening. The room was filled with the strong beat of drums, the resonance of brass, the dramatic precision of saxophones and the improvisation of hot soloists. The audience went wild. After that, the swinging sound took the country by storm, and within months this revived form of jazz passed into the mainstream of American culture.

Teenagers jitterbug their way through 1937's popular Big Apple. Such exhibitionistic dancers, showing off for the crowd, were known as shiners.

The Leaders

Big bands became big business in the late '30s and their leaders were as famous as movie stars. In fact, many band leaders made full-length movies. Benny Goodman appeared in *The Big Broadcast of 1937;* Bob Crosby was featured in *Let's Make Music.* As with other celebrities, lives of the big-band leaders became fair game for gossip-mongers. When the hot-tempered musical brothers Tommy and Jimmy Dorsey feuded over the proper tempo for a song in 1935 and split up the Dorsey Brothers Orchestra, the story was big news. Another hot item was the marriage of band-leader Kay Kyser to his svelte blonde vocalist, Georgia Carroll. Equally well-known among musicians and fans was the notorious Goodman "ray," or stare; Benny Goodman was a perfectionist, and if he turned his "ray" on an underrehearsed musician, the man's days with the band were considered numbered.

The most dedicated swing fans followed the exploits of their heroes in *Downbeat* and *Metronome,* the trade journals of the popular band musicians. Every year both magazines asked readers to write in the names of their favorite bands. The two polls made a distinction between "sweet" bands, which played the schmaltzy sound popularized by the likes of Guy Lombardo, and swing bands, those with a hard-driving beat and improvised solos. The men at right were the top 10 swing band leaders of 1939 as selected in *Metronome.*

1. Benny Goodman

"Metronome's" top band leader, the clarinet-playing Goodman was celebrated as "The King of Swing."

2. Artie Shaw

Shaw, though not as hot a clarinetist as Goodman, had a band many fans rated as swinging as Benny's.

3. Tommy Dorsey

After breaking with his brother Jimmy, trombonist Tommy created a new band with a brassier sound.

4. Bob Crosby

Bing's kid brother, Bob Crosby, sang with the Dorseys before he left to lead a popular Dixieland band.

5. Glenn Miller

An excellent arranger, trombonist Glenn Miller played music noted for fast tempos and lead clarinets.

7. Jimmy Dorsey

Playing both alto sax and clarinet, Jimmy wavered between Dixieland and the more modern swing sound.

9. Jimmie Lunceford

Lunceford's group was one of the decade's most dynamic bands, with its showmanship and bouncy beat.

6. Count Basie

Basie's 15-man band featured great vocalists like Jimmy Rushing and the Count's own droll piano style.

8. Harry James

At first a trumpet soloist with Goodman, James started his own group in 1939—with Benny's backing.

10. Duke Ellington

A gifted composer, the Duke created a sophisticated style using a jazz sound he called "jungle music."

Martha Tilton

Known as "Liltin' Martha Tilton," she made "And the Angels Sing" a hit record in 1939 with Benny Goodman.

Helen O'Connell

Famous as Jimmy Dorsey's canary, swing fans voted her the top female vocalist of 1940, when she was twenty.

Billie Holiday

The great jazz vocalist Billie Holiday was almost unknown when she joined the Artie Shaw Orchestra in 1938.

Canaries and Hits

Almost all the big bands, swing and sweet alike, featured vocalists, usually female. The hot voices—or cool looks—of these singers (*aficionados* called them canaries) often outdid the orchestras in putting across hit tunes. Above is a lineup of canaries of the late '30s and at right are box scores from the entertainment newspaper *Variety* of the top 15 tunes from 1936 to 1940. As the charts show, many of the most popular songs of the swing age were not strictly swing.

1936

ALL MY EGGS IN ONE BASKET
ALONE
CHAPEL IN THE MOONLIGHT
DID I REMEMBER?
IS IT TRUE WHAT THEY SAY ABOUT DIXIE?
IT'S A SIN TO TELL A LIE
LIGHTS OUT
MOON OVER MIAMI
THE MUSIC GOES 'ROUND AND 'ROUND
ON THE BEACH AT BALI BALI
PENNIES FROM HEAVEN
RED SAILS IN THE SUNSET
THE WAY YOU LOOK TONIGHT
WHEN DID YOU LEAVE HEAVEN?
WHEN I'M WITH YOU

1937

BOO HOO
CHAPEL IN THE MOONLIGHT
HARBOR LIGHTS
IT LOOKS LIKE RAIN
LITTLE OLD LADY
MOONLIGHT AND SHADOWS
MY CABIN OF DREAMS
ONCE IN A WHILE
SAILBOAT IN THE MOONLIGHT
SEPTEMBER IN THE RAIN
SO RARE
THAT OLD FEELING
VIENI VIENI
WHEN MY DREAMBOAT COMES HOME
YOU CAN'T STOP ME FROM DREAMING

Mildred Bailey

Singing ballads such as "Willow Weep for Me," Mildred was the top attraction for her husband Red Norvo's band.

Marion Hutton

Blonde Marion Hutton was a vocalist for Glenn Miller. At this time her sister, Betty Hutton, was also a singer.

Ella Fitzgerald

Discovered in an amateur show at age 17, Ella joined Chick Webb and dazzled fans with "A-Tisket A-Tasket."

1938

ALEXANDER'S RAGTIME BAND
A-TISKET A-TASKET
BEI MIR BIST DU SCHÖN
CATHEDRAL IN THE PINES
HEIGH-HO
I'VE GOT A POCKETFUL OF DREAMS
LOVE WALKED IN
MUSIC, MAESTRO, PLEASE!
MY REVERIE
ROSALIE
SAYS MY HEART
THANKS FOR THE MEMORY
THERE'S A GOLD MINE IN THE SKY
TI-PI-TIN
WHISTLE WHILE YOU WORK

1939

AND THE ANGELS SING
BEER BARREL POLKA
DEEP IN A DREAM
DEEP PURPLE
JEEPERS CREEPERS
MAN WITH THE MANDOLIN
MOON LOVE
MY PRAYER
OVER THE RAINBOW
PENNY SERENADE
SUNRISE SERENADE
THREE LITTLE FISHIES
UMBRELLA MAN
WISHING
YOU MUST HAVE BEEN A BEAUTIFUL BABY

1940

BLUEBERRY HILL
CARELESS
FERRYBOAT SERENADE
GOD BLESS AMERICA
I'LL NEVER SMILE AGAIN
IN AN OLD DUTCH GARDEN
INDIAN SUMMER
MAKE BELIEVE ISLAND
OH JOHNNY
ONLY FOREVER
PLAYMATES
SCATTERBRAIN
SOUTH OF THE BORDER
WHEN YOU WISH UPON A STAR
WOODPECKER SONG

Completely swept up by the beat of the Big Apple, a hefty adolescent firmly plants her saddle shoes in a spraddle-legged maneuver called Posin'.

Swinging Dance

"Praise Allah, Wiggle, wiggle, wiggle —/ Praise Allah, Wiggle and dance; / Do that stomp with lots of pomp and sweet romance! / Big Apple, Big Apple—" Lee David and John Redmond conjured up these lyrics in 1937 for a swing dance that quickly became a national craze: the Big Apple. Although the Big Apple remained a total mystery to conservative adults, they nonetheless did their solemn best to try to explain it *(excerpt below)*.

*D*anced in a circle by a group, the Big Apple is led by one who calls the steps, as in a Virginia reel. Fundamental step is a hop similar to the Lindy Hop. In the words of "Variety," "it requires a lot of floating power and fannying." In groups or singly, the dancers follow the caller and combine such steps as the Black Bottom, "shag," Suzi-Q, Charleston, "truckin'," as well as old square-dance turns like London Bridge, and a formation which resembles an Indian Rain Dance. The Big Apple invariably ends upon a somewhat reverent note, with everybody leaning back and raising his arms heavenward. This movement is called "Praise Allah." Through it all, the "caller" shouts continuously—"Truck to the right . . . Reverse it . . . To the left . . . Stomp that right foot . . . Swing it."

TIME MAGAZINE, 1937

Jive Talk

The fast-moving world of swing gave birth to a language called "jive" that was as free and impressionistic and, to the uninitiated, as confusing as the music itself. Below is an abridged dictionary of this lingo, and at right some of the terms are illustrated.

ALLIGATOR—A devotee of swing.

CANARY—A girl vocalist.

CATS—Musicians in a swing orchestra.

CORN, MICKEY MOUSE, SCHMALTZ, SWEET—Uninspired music good only for sedate dancing.

CUTTIN' THE RUG—Dancing to swing music.

DISC OR PLATTER—A recording.

EIGHTY-EIGHT OR MOTHBOX—A piano.

HEPCAT—A very knowledgeable swing fan.

HIDE OR SKINS—Drums, played by a *skin-beater*.

ICKIE—A person who does not understand swing.

IN THE GROOVE—Carried away by good swing.

JAM SESSION—Informal gathering at which swing musicians play for their own pleasure.

JITTERBUG—A dancer responding to swing music.

KICKING OUT—Being very free, improvising.

KNOCKED OUT—To be so engrossed in the music as to blot out all else; a superlative of *sent*, which means to be aroused by the music.

LICORICE STICK—A clarinet.

LONG HAIR—In general an unaware person, musically one who prefers symphonic music.

ONE NIGHTER—A one-night engagement, often with low, or *coffee-and-cake*, wages.

PAPER MAN—A musician who plays by the *spots* (notes) and is incapable of improvising.

PLUMBING—A trumpet, played by a *liver-lips*.

SCAT SINGER—A vocalist who improvises lyrics, substituting nonsense syllables for words.

SWING—Unrestrained but melodic big-band jazz with a strong element of improvisation.

Lindy hoppers kick out

Fats Waller hits the mothbox

Picking a platter to spin

Canaries all: the Andrews Sisters

Cats jam with Duke Ellington around an eighty-eight

Silly Senders

In the '30s, a spate of nonsense songs swept the country. Some, like the best-sellers below, had lyrics so obscure that many fans never did catch on, and they simply faked the words. Thus *"Bei Mir Bist Du Schön"* often became "My Mere Bits of Shame."

BEI MIR BIST DU SCHÖN
Bei Mir Bist Du Schön—
Please let me explain,
Bei Mir Bist Du Schön
means that you're grand,
Bei Mir Bist Du Schön—Again I'll explain,
It means you're the fairest in the land....

TUTTI FRUTTI
Be a rooty-tooty;
Find yourself a cutie,
Why should you be snooty.
Just take your cutie, sweet patootie,
While you have a Tut-ti Frut-ti.
Go to the nearest Sugar Bowl,
Do yourself a favor.
Get a taste of what I mean
S'got the mostest, bestest flavor.
Tut-ti Frut-ti Frut-ti
Tut-ti Frut-ti Frut-ti
Tut-ti Frut-ti Frut-ti

THREE LITTLE FISHIES
Down in de meddy in a itty bitty poo,
Fam fee itty fitty and a mama fitty, foo.
"Fim," fed de mama fitty, "Fim if oo tan,"
And dey fam and dey fam all over de dam.
Boop boop dit-tem dat-tem what-tem Chu!
Boop boop dit-tem dat-tem what-tem Chu!
Boop boop dit-tem dat-tem what-tem Chu!
And dey fam all over de dam.

THE FLAT FOOT FLOOGEE
There's a new killer diller
There's a new Harlem thriller
A new way to ruin the rugs
A new dance for Jitter Bugs.
The Flat Foot Floogee with the Floy Floy
The Flat Foot Floogee with the Floy Floy
The Flat Foot Floogee with the Floy Floy
Floy Doy, Floy Doy, Floy Doy, Floy Doy;
The Flat Foot Floogee with the Flou Flou
The Flat Foot Floogee with the Flou Flou
The Flat Foot Floogee with the Flou Flou,
Flou Dow, Flou Dow, Flou Dow, Flow Dow.

Skin-beater Gene Krupa pounds out the rhythm

A knocked-out alligator

Schmaltzmen play for ickies

Cuttin' the rug

Hepcat in the groove

Jiving it up on their way to class, a bunch of hep high school students in Iowa City practice "truckin'," a finger-waving, hip-tossing walk.

Main Street

Old cronies pass a quiet Saturday afternoon in Versailles, Kentucky.

Two Thirds of a Nation

The big world outside now is so filled with confusion. It seemed to me that hope, in the present muddle, was to try thinking small.　　　SHERWOOD ANDERSON IN *HOME TOWN*

The most striking quality of life in mid-Depression America was summed up by President Roosevelt in his Second Inaugural Address in 1937: "I see one third of the nation ill-housed, ill-clad, ill-nourished." But for the nation's luckier two thirds, the advent of hard times was not quite so devastating, and many people were able to go on about the business of living pretty much as always.

In thousands of small towns all over America, neither Depression-time blues nor the federal government's massive efforts to shoo those blues away really altered the deep-grained texture of community life. Even in the toughest years, Main Street kept its traditional optimism. "What depression?" asked an Indiana businessman in 1935. "We haven't had a depression here." There was even a brief reverse migration as Americans for the first time in decades moved out of the cities and back to the small towns from which they had originally come.

The bad times made some differences, of course. Fewer people bought houses, washing machines or fancy new clothes. Hard-pressed Americans read more borrowed library books and bought fewer newspapers. And instead of spending money on new cars, people made their old ones last, driving them farther and harder. Partly as a re-sult, the number of auto repair shops and gasoline stations doubled during the Depression.

Furthermore, as militant labor unions made the five-day week universal, even the people with steady jobs found they had more leisure time. They also discovered that many of the best things in life were indeed free—or nearly so. For example, bridge-playing, stamp-collecting and listening to the radio all saw an upsurge of popularity. So, too, did such venerable arts and crafts as horseshoe pitching and riding a rocking chair on the front porch.

While the lucky two thirds were thus engaged in living, the federal government launched a massive project to record the overall plight of the nation. As part of this effort, the Farm Security Administration sent out a team of crack photographers, primarily to document rural poverty. While the cameramen indeed took the assigned pictures of barren fields and hungry children, they also turned their cameras on the more common scenes—on people going to church, gossiping on the lawn, eating a roadside picnic. Matched with the words of Thomas Wolfe, E.B. White and other commentators on American life, they add up to a powerful testament, shown on these pages, of the enduring qualities of hometown America at ebb tide.

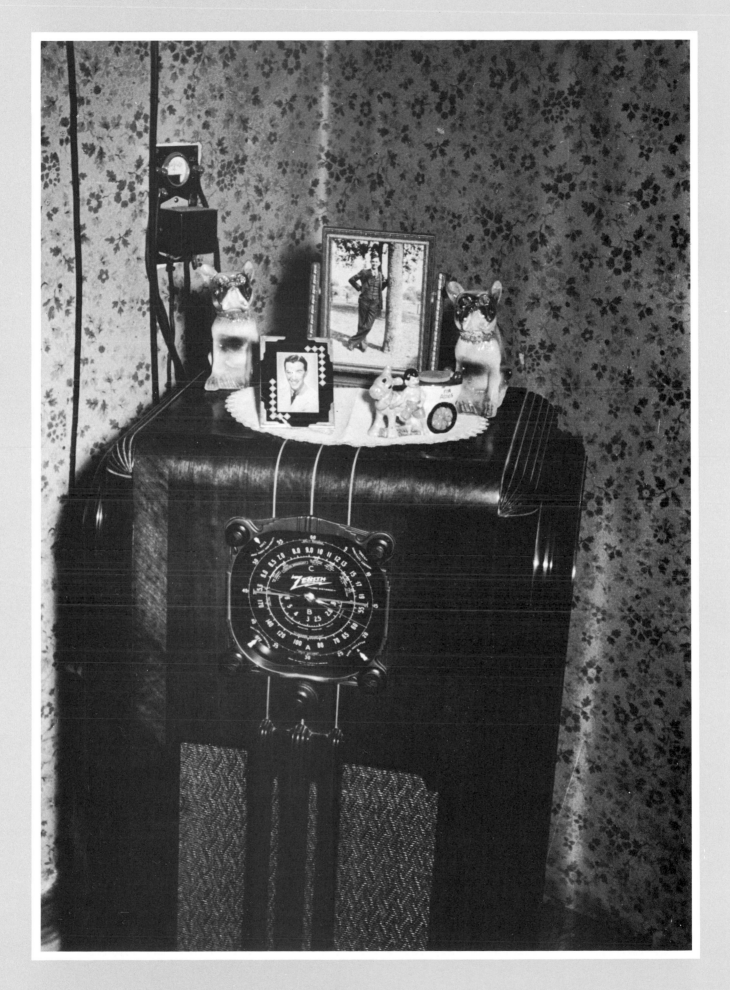

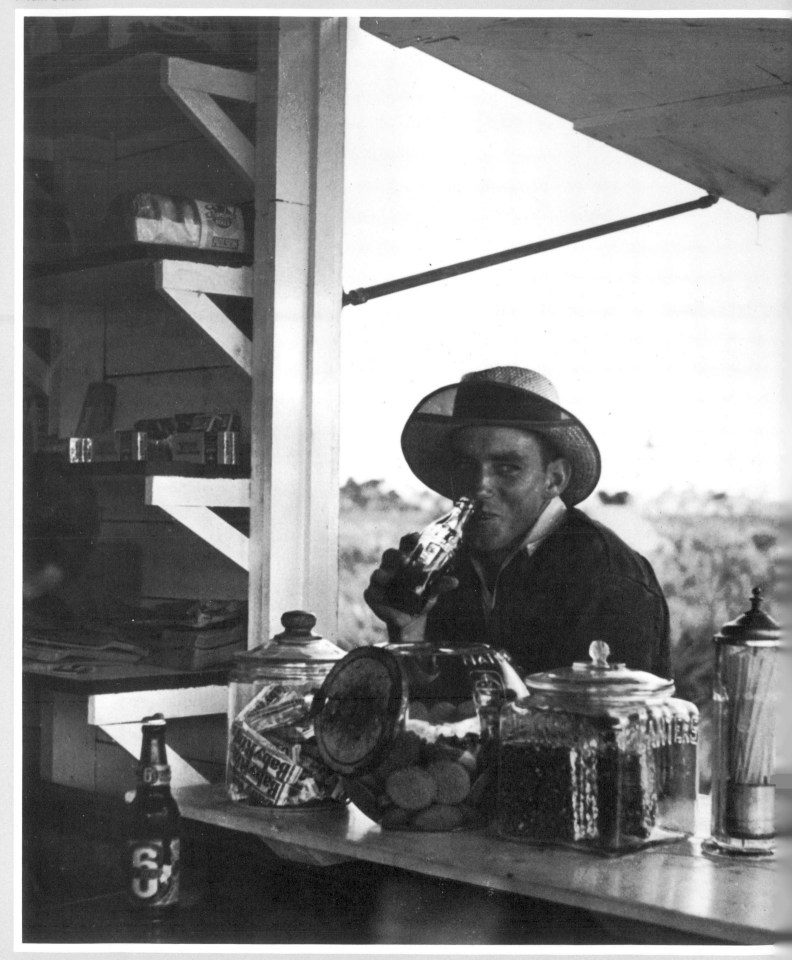

Main Street, like this one in Pennsylvania, seemed
never to change. Thomas Wolfe found
its buildings "all common and familiar as my breath."

A Florida man sips a Coke at the sort of hamburger
stand John Steinbeck lovingly described,
with its "pies in wire cages and oranges in pyramids
of four," and its "coffee urns, shiny and
steaming, with glass showing the coffee level."

In Teton County, Montana, three young members
in good standing of the local Four-H club
show the baby calves that they feed and care for.

An auto repair shop in Atlanta, Georgia: "They
keep the radio going low at the village garage," wrote
E.B. White. "Everything is sort of cozy
and quiet in there, with the music faintly in your ears."

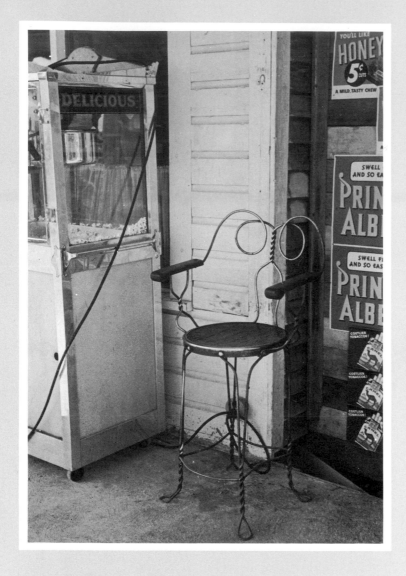

*In Cook, Minnesota, a vacant stool stands
watch beside a nearly empty popcorn machine.*

*Louisiana newsboys fold the local paper, which,
wrote Sherwood Anderson, might tell briefly
of "a revolution in Spain," but "if Mr. Morley's little
girl gets bitten by a dog, it's worth a column."*

"People talking, laughing, streaming out from the dutiful, weekly walnut disinfection of their souls," Wolfe wrote of churchgoers like these in Ohio, people moving "into bright morning-gold of Sunday light again, and standing then in friendly and yet laughing groups upon the lawn outside."

In Lowell, Vermont, a storekeeper lounging
contentedly in his rocker typifies the
rural New Englanders whom Sinclair Lewis called
"a complicated, reticent, slyly humorous lot."

A soda jerk in Corpus Christi, Texas, works
with the sort of panache that prompted Carl Sandburg
to write: "One movie star arches her
eyebrows and refers to 'my public.' One soda-jerker
arches his eyebrows, curves malt-milk
from shaker to glass and speaks of 'my public.' "

"On Sunday afternoon the small town man gets his car out," observed Sherwood Anderson. Here the family auto doubles as an al fresco dining room for these visitors to a community sing at Pie Town, New Mexico.

"The sins of Kalamazoo are neither scarlet nor crimson," Carl Sandburg once said of such city-bred
amusements as the local burlesque; this one is in the outskirts of Washington, D.C.

Hard times or no, a Pennsylvania housewife kept her larder well stocked. "The vision of milk and honey, it comes and goes," wrote E.B. White. "But the odor of cooking goes on forever."

Turned out in their Sunday best, three Louisiana girls try their luck at the bingo tent at that most venerable of rural institutions, the state fair.

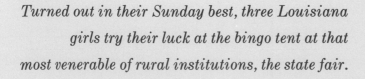

Two boys, clutching books and lunch pails,
come home from school in Hightstown, New Jersey.

"These two sat as if formally, or as if sculptured," was
James Agee's description of two small-town
Americans, "all the while communicating thoroughly
with each other by no outward sign of
word or glance or turning, but by emanation."

Waving in queasy triumph, the winner of a pie-eating contest in Kansas identifies himself while the other contestants battle for second place.

A coal miner and his wife in West Virginia spend an evening by the radio. As E.B. White said, when rural people refer to "The Radio," they mean "a pervading and somewhat godlike presence which has come into their lives and homes."

An ice cream stand in Connecticut recalls Nathanael West's remark about such architectural fantasies:

"Their desire to startle was so eager and guileless . . . it is easy to sigh."

A sphere and needle dominate the New York World's Fair.

Merry Days at Mad Meadow

Here is the magnificent spectacle of a luminous world, apparently suspended in space . . .
OFFICIAL FAIR GUIDE BOOK

. . . and your fellow fairgoers trudge on numbed feet with dazed eyes.
LIFE, JULY 3, 1939

The New York World's Fair was the biggest, giddiest, costliest and most ambitious international exposition ever put on. Even before it opened, on April 30, 1939, amid a blaze of fireworks and a blast of windy publicity, it had cost more than $150 million. Its 1,216-acre grounds in Flushing Meadow, Queens, had been made to order by filling in the entire Queens city dump and planting it with 10,000 trees and one million tulips from Holland. Upon this tract had been built 300 massive, futuristic buildings to house the Fair's 1,500 exhibitors. They included 33 states, 58 foreign countries and 1,300 business firms, ranging from the Ford Motor Company to Dr. Scholl's Footease, which maintained an emergency clinic to treat fairgoers whose arches had sagged along the exposition's 65 miles of paved streets and footpaths.

The Fair's president, gardenia-wearing Grover Aloysius Whalen, had christened this gigantic conglomeration "The World of Tomorrow" and dedicated it to both the blessings of democracy and the wonders of technology. The latter included such marvels as television, nylon stockings, a robot named Elektro that could talk and puff a cigarette, nude statues with titles like Freedom of Assembly, and at the Fair's Theme Centre, the 700-foot-tall needlelike Trylon and the 200-foot globe called the Perisphere.

Mixed in with the technological marvels, the Fair's 45 million visitors found a bewildering assortment of promotional gimmicks, side shows and downright corn, which prompted *The New York Times's* Meyer Berger to refer to the Fair as "Mad Meadow." "See me get milked on a merry-go-round!" shouted the poster hawking Elsie, the Borden Cow, and sure enough, at the Borden exhibit you could see 150 of Elsie's sisters being spun on a revolving milking platform. If you were unlucky, you might hit Elsie on her birthday and hear a squad of Western Union boys deliver a singing telegram: "Mooey Birthday to You." At Ford there was a floor show entitled "A Thousand Times Neigh," a horse's-eye view of the automobile, and Life Savers offered a sky dive *(opposite)*. You could even take in a skin show and ogle an innocent (nearly nude) maiden as she wrestled with Oscar the Obscene Octopus in "Twenty Thousand Legs Under the Sea."

In its two-year run, in fact, the Fair provided just about everything for everybody. "It was the paradox of all paradoxes," wrote Sidney M. Shalett in *Harper's* magazine in 1940. "It was good, it was bad; it was the acme of all crazy vulgarity, it was the pinnacle of all inspiration."

High point of the Fair's Amusement Area was the 250-foot parachute jump, which in two years thrilled two million riders.

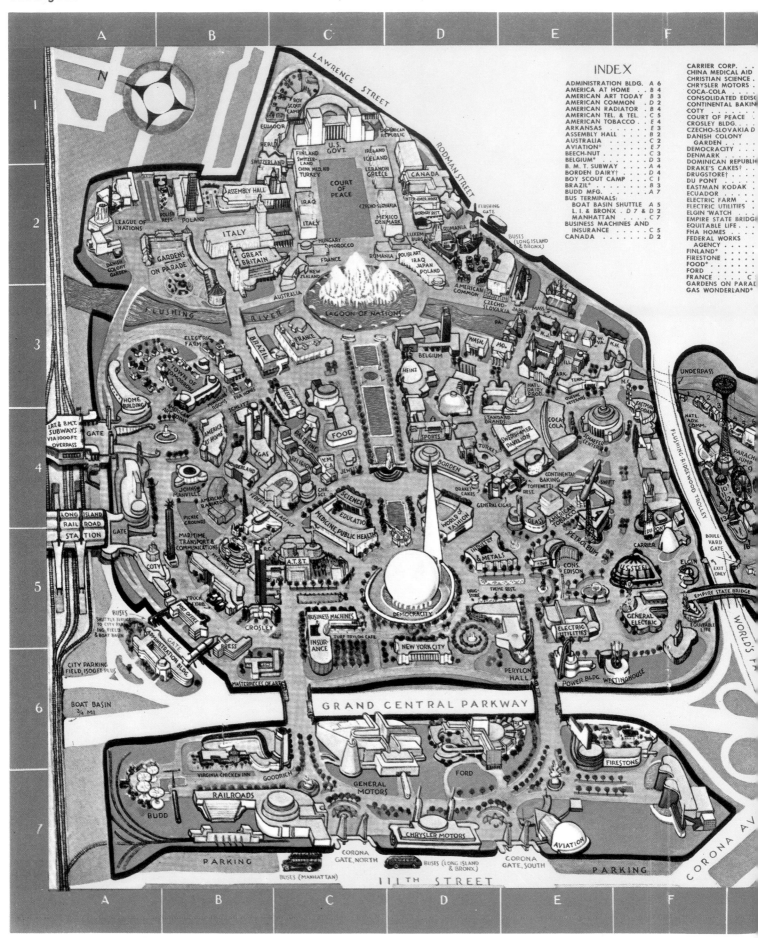

Confronted with the Fair's labyrinth of streets, plazas and buildings, a trio of bewildered matrons asks directions from a uniformed girl guide.

Atop the modernistic Italian Pavilion, the goddess Roma holds court.

Eighty-foot ships' prows flank the entrance to Marine Transportation.

Beneath Poland's 141-foot tower was a restaurant that served Polish vo

Symbols of Socialism at the Soviet Pavilion included "Big Joe," a 30-ton statue of a worker brandishing a red star.

At the National Cash Register Building, a gigantic revolving till rings up the day's attendance at the World's Fair.

Do-it-yourself glass blowing, which enticed millions of visitors to the Glass Center, usually ended in a scary but harmless pop when the bubble burst.

Gimmicks and Giveaways

Not only was it the biggest fair ever, it was also the most expensive for the patrons. Just getting in cost 50 cents, and dinner at the French Pavilion might run as high as $10 a head. Nevertheless, some of the best things at the Fair were free, beginning with morning coffee at the Silex exhibit and ending with the nightly fireworks at the Lagoon of Nations. Betweentimes, without paying a cent, you could choose from among more than 50 movies, for example, the Petroleum Industry's "Oil Can and Does," or the Planters Nut & Chocolate Company's "Mr. Peanut and His Family Tree." Courtesy of Bell Telephone you

could ring up your mother in Seattle. You could also feast on soup and pickles at Heinz, get a shave at Remington Rand, study French at the Linguaphone Institute, ride in a Ford on the Road of Tomorrow and fashion your own Fair souvenir at the Glass Center *(above)*.

In addition, most exhibits handed out prefabricated mementos *(opposite)*. Thus a "Time for Saraka" pin helped you remember an animated cartoon extolling a leading laxative, and a "Where's Elsie?" button meant that you had looked for, and probably found, the famous Borden Cow, in a box stall disguised as a frilly four-poster bed.

JUNGLELAND

G.M. FUTURAMA

HEINZ DOME

SARAKA

CALIFORNIA SOUVENIR

WESTINGHOUSE

BAKELITE

AC SPARK PLUG

PLANTERS NUT CO.

MANUFACTURERS TRUST

FLORIDA PAVILION

TAYLOR HAM

BORDEN

AVIATION SOUVENIR

ADMINISTRATION BUILDING

G.E. BUILDING

SOVIET PAVILION

ITALIAN PAVILION

SWIFT & CO.

SHEFFIELD FARMS

Exhibition souvenirs, either given out free or sold for pennies, helped visitors remember what it was, exactly, that they had seen at the Fair.

A million volts of man-made lightning, accompanied by the crash of synthetic thunder, astounds spectators at the General Electric exhibit.

Wonders of Science

The displays of science-based industry were both dazzling and spooky. Spookiest was the time capsule, designed to preserve for some 50 centuries such items as:

ARTICLES OF COMMON USE

ALARM CLOCK
CAN OPENER
MINIATURE CAMERA
TAPE MEASURE AND SAFETY PIN
TOOTHBRUSH AND TOOTH POWDER
HAT BY LILLY DACHÉ
MICKEY MOUSE PLASTIC CUP
SAFETY RAZOR AND BLADES

MATERIALS OF OUR DAY

FABRICS OF ASBESTOS AND GLASS
CARBON AND STAINLESS STEELS
ANTHRACITE COAL
PLASTIC AIRPLANE CONTROL PULLEY

MISCELLANEOUS ITEMS

SILVER DOLLAR, HALF DOLLAR
   AND OTHER U.S. COINS
ELECTRIC WALL SWITCH AND LAMP SOCKET
THE ALPHABET, IN HANDSET TYPE
SPECIAL MESSAGES FROM SCIENTISTS
   AND WRITERS
VIEWER FOR EXAMINING MICROFILM
   AND NEWSREEL FILM

MICROFILM SEQUENCES

THE LORD'S PRAYER IN 300 LANGUAGES
DICTIONARIES, STANDARD AND SLANG
PHOTOGRAPHS OF FACTORIES
   AND PRODUCTION LINES
ARROWSMITH BY SINCLAIR LEWIS AND *GONE*
   WITH THE WIND BY MARGARET MITCHELL
PHOTOGRAPHS OF POKER PLAYING; A GOLF
   MATCH; A BASEBALL GAME
ASSORTED MAGAZINES
ASSORTED COMIC STRIPS, ATLASES,
   TECHNICAL MANUALS

NEWSREELS

SPEECH BY PRESIDENT
   FRANKLIN D. ROOSEVELT
SCENES FROM HOWARD HUGHES'
   ROUND-THE-WORLD FLIGHT
JESSE OWENS WINNING THE 100-METER DASH IN
   THE OLYMPIC GAMES OF 1936
THE BOMBING OF CANTON IN THE WAR
   BETWEEN CHINA AND JAPAN
THE UNITED STATES NAVY ON MANEUVERS
A FASHION SHOW IN MIAMI, FLORIDA
PREVIEW SCENES OF
   THE NEW YORK WORLD'S FAIR OF 1939

Westinghouse time capsule, to be disinterred in 6939 A.D., hangs between the company's chairman (left) and Fair President Grover Whalen.

Long lines of fairgoers inch their way into General Motors' "Futurama." Despite an hour's wait for admission, 5,100,000 saw the show in one year.

The Shape of Tomorrow

The Fair's "World of Tomorrow" theme received its most spectacular treatment in General Motors' "Futurama." Crowds averaging 28,000 came each day to see the world's largest animated scale model (.8 of an acre), which presented designer Norman Bel Geddes' conception of the American landscape in the year 1960. Each visitor, seated in an armchair on a conveyor belt, was carried over the model on a 15-minute tour, while a sound device in the back of his chair described the scenes he saw below him. The display was so striking that LIFE magazine expanded upon the extravagant GM prophecies in an enthusiastic article excerpted below and on the pages that follow.

America in 1960 is full of a tanned and vigorous people who in 20 years have learned how to have fun. They camp in the forests and hike along the upcountry roads with their handsome wives and children. The college class of 1910 is out there hiking, half its members alive and very fit. These people do not care much for possessions. They are not attached to their own homes and home towns, because trains, express highways (and of course planes) get them across America in 24 hours.

When Americans of 1960 take their two-month vacations, they drive to the great parklands on giant express highways. A two-way skein consists of four 50-m.p.h. lanes on each of the outer edges; two pairs of 75-m.p.h. lanes and in the center, two lanes for 100-m.p.h. express traffic. Cars change from lane to lane at specified intervals, on signal from spaced control towers which can stop and start all traffic by radio. Being out of its driver's control, each car is safe against accident. The cars, built like raindrops, are powered by rear engines that are probably im-

An imagined 1960 airport, serving a small town in the Futurama model, has circular elevators taking airplanes to and from subterranean hangars.

provements of the Diesel. Inside, they are air-conditioned. They cost as low as $200. Off the highway, the driver dawdles again at his own speed and risk.

The highways skirt the great cities. But the happiest people live in one-factory farm-villages producing one small industrial item and their own farm produce. Strip planting protects the valley fields against erosion. The land is really greener than it was in 1939. Federal laws forbid the wanton cutting of wooded hillsides. Dams and canals prevent freshets and floods. Fewer acres, intensively and chemically cultivated, feed all the citizens of the U.S. More of the surface of the land is in forest and park.

Behind this visible America of 1960, hidden in the laboratories, are the inventors and engineers. By the spring of 1939 they had cracked nearly every frontier of progress. Liquid air is by 1960 a potent, mobile source of power. Atomic energy is being used cautiously. Power is transmitted by radio beams, focused by gold reflectors. The Lanova Cell has made all gas-

oline motors Diesels. These great new powers make life in 1960 immensely easier. Such new alloys as heat-treated beryllium bronze give perfect service. Great telescopes show 100 times more of the cosmos than the men of 1939 saw in the sky. Cures for cancer and infantile paralysis have extended man's life span and his wife's skin is still perfect at the age of 75. Architecture and plane construction have been revolutionized by light, noninflammable, strong plastics from soybeans. Houses are light, graceful, easily replaced. Electronic microscopes literally see everything.

On every front America in 1960 knows more about unleashing the best energies in its citizens. Nearly everyone is a high-school graduate. The talented get the best education in the world. More people are interested in life, the world, themselves and in making a better world. Politics and emotion still slow progress. But these obstructions are treated with dwindling patience in 1960.

LIFE, JUNE 5, 1939

In the city of 1960, 1,500-foot-high office buildings and apartment houses form self-sufficient sub-cities set alongside 14-lane superhighways.

The smash hit at the Fair was Billy Rose's Aquacade, where eight million visitors saw a team of "Aquafemmes" splash about to waltz music.

Text Credits

23—Will Rogers quote: Will Rogers, *How We Elect Our Presidents*, Donald Day, ed., Little, Brown and Co., 1952, p. 111. 35-37—"Invasion from Mars" by Howard Koch. Reprinted by permission of author and Manheim Fox Enterprises. 1938, 1940, 1967, 1969 Copyright Howard Koch. 38—"Amos and Andy" script written by Freeman Gosden and Charles Correll, supplied by Jim Harmon, Hollywood, California. Used by permission of Columbia Broadcasting System. 39 —Kaltenborn broadcast from H.V. Kaltenborn, *I Broadcast the Crisis*, New York, Random House, 1938. 48—Auto worker quote adapted from *The New Republic*, March 18, 1931, pp. 118-119. 51—Kentucky miner quote from *The Nation*, June 8, 1932, p. 651. 57—Tennessee squatter quote adapted from *These Are Our Lives*, by the Federal Writers' Project, Works Progress Administration, University of North Carolina Press, 1939, pp. 375-376. 70—Migratory worker's log book adapted from *Brother Can You Spare A Dime?* Milton Meltzer, Alfred A. Knopf, 1969, p. 140. 79—"Little Orphan Annie Song" courtesy of Ovaltine Food Products. 83 —"Have You Tried Wheaties." Lyrics by Donald D. Davis and music by M.K. Jerome. Music copyright 1919 by General Mills, Inc. Copyright renewed 1946. Lyrics copyright 1939 by General Mills, Inc. Used by permission—"Wave the Flag for Hudson High." Lyrics by David Owen and music by Phillip R. Culkin. Copyright 1940 by General Mills, Inc. Used by permission. 123—Walter Lippmann quotes: New York *Herald Tribune*, April 28, 1932; *Review of Reviews*, May 1933 —Will Rogers quotes: *The Autobiography of Will Rogers*, Donald Day, ed., Houghton Mifflin Co., 1949, pp. 312-313; *How We Elect Our Presidents*, Donald Day, ed., Little, Brown and Co., 1952, pp. 143-144, 148-149. 124—F.D.R. to Dan Roper: D.C. Roper, "The New Deal Endorses Profits," *Forum*, Dec. 1934; H.L. Mencken quote: "Three Years of Dr. Roosevelt," *American Mercury*, March 1936. 126

—Fireside Chat: *The Public Papers and Addresses of Franklin D. Roosevelt*, Volume Two, "The Year of Crisis: 1933," Random House, 1938, pp. 61-65. 136, 137—Pro-F.D.R. materials: Richard Harrity & Ralph G. Martin, *The Human Side of F.D.R.*, Duell, Sloan & Pearce, 1960, p. 181; Dixon Wecter, *The Age of the Great Depression*, Macmillan, 1948, p. 96; Ben Whitehurst, *"Dear Mr. President,"* E.P. Dutton & Co., 1937, pp. 17, 34—Anti-F.D.R. materials: Letters, Franklin D. Roosevelt Library, Hyde Park, N.Y.—Message from Hearst executive: James MacGregor Burns, *Roosevelt: The Lion and the Fox*, Harcourt, Brace & World, 1956, p. 241—Pegler quote: Westbrook Pegler, *The Dissenting Opinions of Mister Westbrook Pegler*, Charles Scribner's Sons, 1938, pp. 38-40. 139—"The Cliché Expert Testifies as a Roosevelt Hater," Copyright by Frank Sullivan. Reprinted by permission of the author. 215—Huey Long quotes: Huey P. Long, *My First Days in the White House*, Telegraph Press, Harrisburg, Pa., 1935. 216—Father Coughlin quotes: *New York Times*, March 4, 1935; July 17, 1936; TIME magazine, October 5, 1936; *New York Times*, November 21, 1938. 220—Wilfred Mendelson letters: *Let My People Know*, Joseph Leeds, ed., New York, 1942. 239—"Bei Mir Bist Du Schön," Secunda-Jacobs-Chan-Chaplin. © 1937 by Harms, Inc. Used by permission of Warner Bros.-Seven Arts Music. All rights reserved—"Tutti Frutti," Doris Fisher and Slim Gaillard. Copyright 1938 by Anne-Rachel Music Corporation. Copyright renewed 1965 and assigned to Anne-Rachel Music Corporation and Fred Fisher Music Co., Inc.—"Three Little Fishies," Saxie Dowell. Copyright 1939 by Anne-Rachel Music Corporation. Copyright renewed 1966 and assigned to Anne-Rachel Music Corporation—"The Flat Foot Floogee," Slim Gaillard, Slam Stewart and Bud Green. © 1938, 1966 Jewel Music Publishing Co., Inc. at 1619 Broadway, N.Y., N.Y. 10019.

Picture Credits

The sources for the illustrations which appear in this book are shown below. Credits for the pictures from left to right are separated by semicolons, from top to bottom by dashes.

Cover—Tom McAvoy.

6,7—Historical Collection Security Pacific National Bank. 8,9—Edholm and Blomgren, Lincoln, Nebraska. 10,11—Library of Congress. 12,13—Brown Brothers. 14, 15—Museum of the City of New York. 16,17—Carl Mydans. 18,19—Al P. Burgert. 20,21—Culver Pictures. 22—Courtesy Halbert F. Speer. 28,29—Culver Pictures. 31—Bettmann Archive. 32—Culver Pictures. 33—Irving Settel; John Phillips; Culver Pictures. 34—Culver Pictures. 38—Culver Pictures. 39—CBS. 40—Irving Settel. 41,42,43—Culver Pictures. 44,45—University of Washington Library. 47 —Brown Brothers. 48—*The Detroit News*. 49—Library of Congress. 50 through 55 —Library of Congress except page 51, Library of Congress, Fred Ward from Black Star. 56,57—Margaret Bourke-White; Library of Congress. 58,59—Margaret Bourke-White. 60,61—Mrs. Henry Rhoades. 62 through 73—Library of Congress. 74, 75—Western Ways Features. 77—Wayne State University, Labor History Archives. 78—Chicago Tribune-New York News Syndicate courtesy Woody Gelman and Nostalgia Press. 79—John Savage courtesy Ernest Trova except bottom left courtesy Woody Gelman, Nostalgia Press, and the Wonder Co. 80—Courtesy Al Williamson, © King Features Syndicate—courtesy Woody Gelman and Nostalgia Press, © King Features Syndicate. 81—Culver Pictures—Al Freni courtesy Douglas Steinbauer, © King Features Syndicate, except bottom right courtesy Woody Gelman and Nostalgia Press, © King Features Syndicate. 82—General Mills, Inc. (2); John Savage courtesy Ernest Trova—General Mills, Inc.—Al Freni courtesy General Mills, Inc. 83—General Mills, Inc.—Al Freni courtesy General Mills, Inc.—General Mills, Inc.; John Savage courtesy Ernest Trova. 84 —Courtesy United Features Syndicate. 85—MGM. 86—John Savage courtesy Ernest Trova except bottom left courtesy Ernest Trova and Ralston Purina Co. 87—John Savage courtesy Ernest Trova. 88,89—Al Freni photographed from the Buck Rogers Collection of Tony Goodstone, New York City. 90—John Savage courtesy Ernest Trova except cartoon Walter Daran courtesy Chicago Tribune-New York News Syndicate. 91—Walter Daran courtesy Chicago Tribune-New York News Syndicate. 92—Courtesy Loraine Burdick except top right Marcus Adams, London. 93—Courtesy Loraine Burdick. 94—Al Freni courtesy Ione Wollenzein; courtesy Loraine Burdick; courtesy Ione Wollenzein. 95,96,97 —Al Freni courtesy Ione Wollenzein. 98,99—*Houston Chronicle*. 101—No credit. 102—Collection of Little Bohemia Lodge, Manitowish Waters, Wisconsin. 103 —United Press International. 104—*Daily Oklahoman* (2); no credit. 105—Wide World. 106—United Press International except top left *Daily Oklahoman*. 107 —Charles Moore from Black Star. 108—Brown Brothers. 114,115—Franklin D.

Roosevelt Library, Hyde Park, New York. 117—Reprinted from *Vanity Fair* (now *Vogue* incorporating *Vanity Fair*), copyright © 1934, 1962 by The Condé Nast Publications Inc. 118—Underwood & Underwood. 119—United Press International except second from right Wide World—*The New York Times* and Wide World courtesy Franklin D. Roosevelt Library, Hyde Park, New York; United Press International; Wide World (2); Keystone View; Wide World; Arthur Griffin—United Press International; Wide World; no credit; United Press International; Wide World; United Press International—United Press International; Wide World; Franklin D. Roosevelt Library, Hyde Park, New York. 120,121—Franklin D. Roosevelt Library, Hyde Park, New York; Underwood & Underwood. 122,123—United Press International. 124,125—Reprinted from *Vanity Fair* (now *Vogue* incorporating *Vanity Fair*), copyright © 1934, 1962 by The Condé Nast Publications Inc. (from Culver Pictures). 127—Reproduced by permission of *Esquire* magazine © 1935 (renewed 1963) by Esquire, Inc. 128—Culver Pictures; Photo World. 129—United Press International. 130,131 —Underwood & Underwood. 132,133—From "Public Building" by Public Works Administration and Federal Works Agency. 134,135—Culver Pictures; National Collection of Fine Arts copied by Henry B. Beville. 138—Drawing by Peter Arno, copyright © 1936, 1964 The New Yorker Magazine, Inc. 140,141—Tom McAvoy. 142,143—W. Eugene Smith from Black Star. 145—United Press International. 146—Culver Pictures. 148—George Karger-Pix. 149—Jerome Zerbe. 150—Wide World—United Press International; Jerome Zerbe; United Press International. 151—Top Wide World (3)—bottom United Press International (2). 152—United Press International. 153—Photo World (Edward Ozern); Culver Pictures—Stork Club; Wide World; Jerome Zerbe. 154,155—Brown Brothers. 156 —Wide World; Underwood & Underwood—Wide World—United Press International. 157—Underwood & Underwood except top right United Press International. 158,159—Culver Pictures. 160,161—Interphoto. 163—Harris & Ewing from the Gilloon Agency. 164,165—Wayne State University, Labor History Archives. 166—Library of Congress. 167—Wide World except bottom United Press International. 168,169—Wayne State University, Labor History Archives. 170, 171—United Press International except top left William Vandivert and top right the Historical Society of Pennsylvania. 173—Drawing by William Gropper. 174, 175—Wide World; Brown Brothers. 177—Library of Congress. 178,179—Historical Collection, Title Insurance and Trust Company, San Diego, California. 181 —Credits for this page are listed according to amount used from each source: United Press International; Wide World; Culver Pictures; Clarence Sinclair Bull-MGM; Paramount Pictures; Ron Partridge from Black Star; 20th Century-

Fox; Rex Hardy. 182,183—Culver Pictures. 184—Collection Herman G. Weinberg. 185—The Bettmann-Springer Film Archive. 186—Culver Pictures; Photo Files—Photo Files; Culver Pictures—The Academy of Motion Picture Arts and Sciences; Culver Pictures; Warner Bros. 187—Bert Six for Warner Bros. 188, 189—Culver Pictures. 190—No credit. 191—Culver Pictures. 192,193—Brown Brothers. 194,195—MGM except bottom right Culver Pictures. 196,197,198 —Culver Pictures. 199—Culver Pictures; MGM. 200,201—Culver Pictures. 202, 203—© Walt Disney Productions. 204—Columbia Pictures; Walter Wanger Productions—Culver Pictures; R.R. Stuart Collection; Culver Pictures—Culver Pictures; The Bettmann Archive; Larry Edmunds Bookshop, Hollywood, California—The Museum of Modern Art Film Stills Archive; The Academy of Motion Picture Arts and Sciences; United Artists—20th Century-Fox; March of Time-Pix; Photo Files. 205—Culver Pictures; Photo Files; Universal Studios —G.E. Richardson for Paramount; Photo Files; Paramount Pictures—Selznick International Pictures, Inc.; Warner Bros.; The Bettmann Archive—Culver Pictures; The Springer-Bettmann Film Archive; Culver Pictures—Forrest J Ackerman Archives; Sherman Clark for Universal Pictures; Culver Pictures. 206 —George Karger-Pix. 207—Culver Pictures except center Atlanta Historical Society. 208,209—© Selznick International Pictures, Inc.© renewed 1967 MGM, Inc. 210,211—Alfred Eisenstaedt-Pix. 213—Otto Hagel. 214—Louisiana State Museum. 217—Wide World. 218—Hans Knopf-Pix. 220,221—Wide World. 222 —Robert Capa. 227—Margaret Bourke-White. 228,229—Popsie, New York. 231 —Otto F. Hess. 232—No credit—Brown Brothers; Ernest R. Smith—The Bettmann Archive. 233—Down Beat magazine; Brown Brothers; Photo Files —Photo Files; Duncan P. Schiedt; Photo Files. 234,235—Popsie, New York except left Down Beat magazine. 236,237—Peter Stackpole. 238—New York Daily News; Duncan P. Schiedt—Hansel Mieth; Richard Merrill—Ernest R. Smith. 239—Duncan P. Schiedt—Pete Culross; United Press International—Photo Files; Bernard Hoffman. 240,241—Ken Johnson. 242 through 265—Library of Congress except page 256—Library of Congress, Fred Ward from Black Star. 266,267 and 269—Frank T. Sobeck. 270,271—Drawing by Carl Rose, copyright © 1940, 1968 by The New Yorker Magazine, Inc.; Dave Scherman. 272,273—Museum of the City of New York—Edward J. Orth courtesy Roy R. Mumma; Edward J. Orth—Frank T. Sobeck. 274—Eric Schaal-Pix. 275—J.R. Eyerman. 276 —Eric Schaal-Pix. 277—Underwood & Underwood. 278,279—General Motors. 280—Gjon Mili. 281—Alfred Eisenstaedt-Pix. 282,283—Edward J. Orth.

Bibliography

Amory, Cleveland, Who Killed Society? Harper & Row, 1960.

Allen, Frederick Lewis, Since Yesterday. Bantam Books, 1965.

Baxter, John, Hollywood in the Thirties. A.S. Barnes & Co., 1968.

Bendiner, Robert, Just Around the Corner. Harper & Row, 1967.

Bird, Caroline, The Invisible Scar. David McKay Co., 1966.

Blum, Daniel, A New Pictorial History of the Talkies. G.P. Putnam's Sons, 1968.

Burns, James MacGregor, Roosevelt: The Lion and the Fox.
    Harcourt, Brace & Co., 1956.

Clarens, Carlos, Horror Films. G.P. Putnam's Sons, 1967.

Coleman, MacAlister, Men and Coal. Farrar & Rinehart, Inc., 1943.

Cook, Frederick J., The F.B.I. Nobody Knows. The Macmillan Company, 1964.

Daniels, Jonathan, The Time Between the Wars. Doubleday & Co., 1966.

Feather, Leonard, The Encyclopedia of Jazz. Rev. ed. Horizon Press, 1968.

Federal Writers' Project, Works Progress Administration, These Are Our Lives.
    University of North Carolina Press, 1939.

Griffith, Richard, and Arthur Mayer, The Movies. Simon & Schuster, 1957.

Gunther, John, Roosevelt in Retrospect. Harper & Bros., 1950.

Halliwell, Leslie, The Filmgoer's Companion. Hill & Wang, 1967.

Harmon, James, The Great Radio Heroes. Ace Books, Inc., 1967.

Hoover, J. Edgar, Persons in Hiding. Little, Brown & Co., 1938.

Howe, Irving, and Lewis Coser, The American Communist Party.
    Beacon Press, 1957.

Kempton, Murray, Part of Our Time. Dell Publishing Co., 1955.

Leonard, Jonathan Norton, Three Years Down. Carrick & Evans, 1939.

Leuchtenburg, William E., Franklin D. Roosevelt and the New Deal.
    Harper & Row, 1963.

Levinson, Edward, Labor on the March. Harper & Bros., 1938.

Maxwell, Elsa, R.S.V.P. Little, Brown & Co., 1954.

Meltzer, Milton, Brother Can You Spare A Dime? Alfred A. Knopf, 1969.

O'Connor, Harvey, Steel-Dictator. The John Day Co., 1935.

Roosevelt, James, and Sidney Shalett, Affectionately, F.D.R.
    Harcourt, Brace & Co., 1959.

Schickel, Richard, The Disney Version. Simon & Schuster, 1968.

Schlesinger, Arthur M., Jr., The Age of Roosevelt. Vol. II: The Coming of the New
    Deal. Vol. III: The Politics of Upheaval. Houghton Mifflin Co., 1958, 1960.

Settel, Irving, A Pictorial History of Radio. Grosset & Dunlap, 1967.

Simon, George T., The Big Bands. The Macmillan Company, 1967.

Taft, Philip, Organized Labor in American History. Harper & Row, 1964.

Tanner, Louise, All the Things We Were. Doubleday & Co., 1968.

Taylor, Deems, A Pictorial History of the Movies. Simon & Schuster, 1949.

Wecter, Dixon, The Age of the Great Depression. The Macmillan Company, 1948.

Whitehead, Donald, The F.B.I. Story. Random House, 1956.

Acknowledgments

The editors of this book wish to thank the following persons and institutions for their assistance:

Forrest J Ackerman, Forrest J Ackerman Archives, Los Angeles; Atlanta Historical Society; A. K. Baragwanath, Senior Curator, Museum of the City of New York; Busby Berkeley, Los Angeles; Larry Booth, Director of Historical Collection, Title Insurance and Trust Company, San Diego; Mrs. Ruth P. Braun, Chief Librarian, The Detroit News; Mrs. Loraine Burdick, Celebrity Doll Club, Puyallup, Washington; Ted Cavagnaro, St. Louis; Mrs. Shirley Clarke, Curator, Audio-Visual Materials, Labor History Archives, Wayne State University, Detroit; Harry Collins, Brown Brothers; Charles Correll and Freeman Gosden, Los Angeles; Patricia Crews, Daily Oklahoman, Oklahoma City; Robert Cunningham, Stillwater, Oklahoma; Virginia Daiker, Prints and Photographs Division, Library of Congress; James H. Davis, Western History Division, Denver Public Library; Frank Driggs, New York City; Cam Duane, Institute of Texan Cultures, San Antonio; Moe Fishman, Secretary, Veterans of the Abraham Lincoln Battalion, New York; Woody Gelman, Nostalgia Press, New York; Dorothy Gimmestad, Assistant Curator, Audio-Visual Library, Minnesota Historical Society, St. Paul; Tony Goodstone, New York City; Chester Gould, The Chicago Tribune; Jim Harmon, Radio Heroes Society, Hollywood, California; Martin Herman, The Philadelphia Bulletin; The Historical Society of Pennsylvania, Philadelphia; Hoblitzelle Theatre Arts Library, University of Texas, Austin; Roy King, Librarian, St. Louis Post Dispatch; Walter Kost, Manager, Consumer and Promotion Services, General Mills Inc., Minneapolis; Joseph W. Marshall, Mrs. Clarice D. Morris, Paul J. McLaughlin, Franklin D. Roosevelt Library, Hyde Park, New York; Robert D. Monroe, Director of Special Collections, University of Washington Library, Seattle; Dan Morgenstern, Down Beat, Chicago; John McCarty, Director, High Plains Art Gallery, Amarillo, Texas; Garnett McCoy, Archivist, Archives of American Art, Detroit; Herbert McLaughlin, Arizona Photographic Associates, Phoenix; Sol Novin, Culver Pictures, New York City; Francis V. O'Connor, University of Maryland; Edward J. Orth, Los Angeles; Margot P. Pearsall, Curator, Social History Division, Detroit Historical Museum; Warner Pflug, Archivist, Labor History Archives, Wayne State University, Detroit; Victor R. Plukas, Security Pacific National Bank, Los Angeles; Henry Raduta, Manager, Chicago Tribune-New York News Syndicate Inc.; Gleason W. Romer, Miami; Marthanne B. Root, Austin; Sy Seidman, New York City; Robert Shipler, Salt Lake City; Mildred Simpson, Librarian, Library of Motion Picture Arts and Sciences, Los Angeles; R. Henderson Shuffler, Director, Institute of Texan Cultures, San Antonio; Ernest Smith, New York City; Paul Smith, President, Johnson Smith Company, Grosse Pointe; Ray Stuart, R. R. Stuart Collection, Los Angeles; Patrick Sullivan, Massachusetts State Library, Boston; Judith Topaz, Assistant, Iconographic Collections, State Historical Society of Wisconsin, Madison; Ernest Trova, St. Louis, Missouri; John Conrad Weiser, New York City; Al Williamson, Callicoon, New York; Mrs. Ione Wollenzein, Waukesha, Wisconsin; Mary Yushak, Museum of Modern Art, New York City; Jerome Zerbe, New York City.

Index